QUALITY CONTROL OF GOODS AND THE PRICING POLICY IN CAMEROON:

A Legal Discourse

GALDA VERLAG 2019

ROLAND DJIEUFACK
MBIFI RICHARD
MARCELOUS NYIAWUNG

QUALITY CONTROL OF GOODS AND THE PRICING POLICY IN CAMEROON:

A Legal Discourse

GALDA VERLAG 2019

Bibliografische Information der Deutschen Nationalbibliothek
Die Deutsche Nationalbibliothek verzeichnet diese Publikation in der Deutschen Nationalbibliografie; detaillierte bibliografische Daten sind im Internet über http://dnb.ddb.de abrufbar.

Direct all inquiries to Galda Verlag, Franz-Schubert-Str. 61, 16548 Glienicke, Germany

ISBN 978-3-96203-096-4 (Print)
ISBN 978-3-96203-097-1 (E-Book)

DEDICATION

To our parents

FOREWORD

Shedding light in '*dark*' areas of contemporary commercial law is becoming the hallmark of the authors. A book on the issues of quality and pricing system of goods in Cameroon (an area of mercantile law not adequately researched on) is very timely. It is justified for addressing the pertinent cases of buyers' dissatisfaction over the poor quality of goods and discriminatory prices in the market. The book is conveniently written at a time when there are incessant complaints from commercial and consumer buyers relating to business malpractices orchestrated by unscrupulous sellers in the Cameroonian market.

The work is therefore a distillation of ideas that have undergone a long period of germination and have been garnered from a wide range of sources. This book reveals the tensions that exist in private law governing commercial transactions between the strictness of contractual obligations and the principle of equity which moderate conduct in business life, between purity and commercial reality.

The authors carefully reiterate the principle of *caveat venditor* in advocating for the fact that the seller is bound to take responsibility for poor quality and the discriminatory prices of goods that are not in conformity with the specifications of the contract of sale and the statutory laws in force.

I have no doubt that our commercial law will rise to these expectations in this realm of technological advancements. I strongly salute these authors for their interest in this complicated area of sale of goods where they have done a good blend of theory and practice. One thing is certain: a book written in English on the OHADA Law will go a long way in elucidating the legitimate needs of the mercantile community in Cameroon.

Irene D. N. Fokum Sama-Lang, Ph.D.
Associate Professor of Laws
Faculty of Laws & Political Science
University of Buea
Cameroon

PREFACE

The primary objective of this book is to promote a favourable business climate and raise the general awareness of buyers of goods in Cameroon.

This study aims at pointing out the hurdles that beset the control of quality and prices of goods sold in the markets by the government of Cameroon. The proliferation of goods in the formal and informal sectors of the economy still poses a challenge over the quality of goods and pricing policy in Cameroon. Sophisticated formal business laws designed to facilitate this task are not effectively implemented deeply even in the informal sector of the economy. Consequently, consumer and commercial buyers of goods do suffer from defects in quality and discriminatory prices of goods and services. Adopting an in-depth content analysis and critical assessment of primary and secondary data, this study advocates for an enhanced enforcement of the laws in place in order to establish a favourable business landscape for investment.

The emphasis today in Cameroon in particular, is towards economic stability geared at improving the economy of the country relating to the conduct of commercial activities. Consumers in Cameroon are incessantly complaining of business malpractices in the market place orchestrated by unscrupulous business people. This is clearly an indication that Cameroonians are becoming more business conscientious and that the Cameroonian business industry is, to some extent, responding adequately to the needs of the economy. Despite the existence of legislations governing commercial activities in general in Cameroon, there is still an urgent need for stakeholders involved in the business sphere to adequately exercise their responsibilities; and it is in response to this duty that this book has been written. In fact, this duty arises when commercial and consumer buyers of goods are vulnerable to poor quality and discriminatory prices of goods in the markets.

In this book, the authors have carefully discussed their viewpoints from a legal perspective. We have drawn from existing literature on commercial law in general in Cameroon, analysed the relevant statutes and elucidated on material drawn from extensive field research work conducted in Cameroon.

The book is in six chapters. Chapter One opens up with a general introduction. Chapter two discusses the concept of pricing. Chapter three examines quality control of goods in the Cameroonian economy. Chapter four examines the control of prices in the Cameroon Economy. Chapter five dwells on the offences and sanctions on illegal and unlawful pricing of products in Cameroon. Chapter six highlights the remedies available to a buyer of goods in the event of a defect in quality.

The book is a useful source of reference for students of Commercial and Consumer Law, legal practitioners who do deal with issues on commercial matters, magistrates and judges, businessmen who actively are involved in the commercial activities and the government. This study will definitely go a long way to offer a better understanding to existing pricing regulations which are mostly enacted in the French language.

This study indeed would not have been conducted without the assistance of many persons who in various ways aided to shape our ideas. We actually had the assistance of some traders operating in the major towns of Bamenda, Douala and Yaoundé in Cameroon. We also register our gratitude to some consumer associations, as well as to some decentralised government institutions, such as the Regional Delegations of Trade in Bamenda and Douala.

We are thus confident that our findings will be a great importance to the stakeholders involved in commercial activities. We humbly accept and take responsibility for all errors and omissions in this book.

Roland Djieufack, Ph.D.

Mbifi Richard, Ph.D.

Marcelous Nyiawung, LL.M.

Bamenda, Cameroon

TABLE OF CONTENTS

THE MEANING OF THE CONCEPT OF PRICING POLICY

QUALITY CONTROL OF GOODS

TABLE OF STATUTES

Statute of Fraud 1677.

Infants Relief Act 1874.

Minors' Contract Act 1987.

Decree No. 88/204 of 5 February 1988, re-organising the Ministry of Commerce.

Arrêté No. 0196/MINCOMMERCE du 13 April 2007 portant fixation de la liste des produits et services dont les prix et tarifs sont soumis a la procédure d'homologation préalable.

Loi-Cadre 2011/012 du 6 mai 2011 portant protection du consommateur au Cameroun.

OHADA Uniform At on General Commercial Law of 15th February 2011.

Law No. 2015/018 of December 21 2015 governing commercial activity in Cameroon.

Civil Codes (CC) of Cameroon, Article 1582 CC; Côte d'Ivoire, Article 1582 CC; France, Article 1582 CC.

LIST OF CASES

Cameroon

Brasseries du Cameroun v. Ambe John, Appeal No. BCA/8/93 March 1994 (Unreported)

*Laborex c/ MejoM'obamMoise,*TGI Mfoundi, n° 246, 432002

Michael Ebwe v. Hubert Euverte Suit No. HCSW/24, 1974, Buea High Court (unreported)

Scholastic Nsaiboti v. Felix Ezeafor, Appeal No. BCA/6/73 of March 1974, Bamenda Court of Appeal (Unreported)

Foreign

Afrotech v. MIA [2001] 6 WRN 65

Andrews Brothers (Bournemouth), Ltd. V. Singer & Co., (1934) 1 K.B

AshingtonPeggeries Ltd v. Chrisptopher Hill Ltd., [1972] AC

Borrowman Phillips & Co v. Free & Hollis(1878) 4 QBD 500

Boshali v. Allied Commercial Exported Ltd., [1961] All N.L.R73

British Steel Corp v. Claveland Bridge and Engineering Co Ltd [1984] 1 ALL ER

Carlill v Carbolic Smoke Ball Company, (1893) + QB 256

Champanthac& Co Ltd v. Waller & Co Ltd., (1979) 1K.B 254

Currie v. Misa (1975) LR 10 Exch 153, 162)

Dunlop Pneumatic Tyre Co v. Selfridge Ltd., [1915] A.C 847

Ernest Friedrischdorf and Co v. Fuja, [1967] LLR 115

Godley v. Perry, [1887] 12 App. Cas. 284

Griffiths v. Peter Conway Ltd., [1939] 1 All ER 685

Hadley v. Baxendale, [1854] 9 Exch 341

Hartog v. Colin & Shields, [1939] 3 ALL ER 566

Henry Kendall & Sons v. William Lillico& Sons, [1911] A.C

Ibedewelu v. Lawal [1971] 1All NLR

Ijomo v. Mid Motors Nigeria Ltd., CCHCJ / 9/ 754

Ingham v. Ernes,(1955) 2Q. B. 366

Khalil and Dibo v. Mastronikolis, [1949] 12 WACA 462

Kleinwort Benson Ltd v. Malaysia Mining Corp Bhd [1989] 1 ALL ER 785

*Lorymer v. Smith, (*1822) 1 B & C 1

Mac Gill v. Tailbot, (2002) GWD 12382

Moody v. Gregson [1868] LR Ex 49

Onutu v. Adeleke and Another[1975] N.L.R. 130

Parkinson v. Lee (1802) 2 East 314, 102 Eng. Rep. 389

Photo Productions Ltd. v. Securicor Transport Ltd.

Reardon Smith Ltd. v. Hansen – Tangen, (1976) 3 All ER 570

Seyers v. Jones, [1848] 154 ER 426

Smith v. Hughes (1871) LR 6 QB 597

Suisse Atlantique Société d'Armement Maritime S.A v. N.V. Rotterdam ScheKolen Centrale, [1967] 1 A.C. 361

Thomas v. Thomas(1842) 2 QB 851

Thornett and Febr v. Beers and Sons, [1919] 1K.B 486

Toépfer v. Continental Grain Co., [1974] 1 Llyod'd Rep.

Universal Vulcanizing (Nig.) Ltd.v. I.U.T.T.C, [1962] NWLR

Warwick v. Mackenzie Co Ltd., [1921] 2 W.N.R

Wilson Smitheett& Cape (Sugar) Ltd v. Bangladesh Sugar & Food Industries Corp. [1986] 1 Lloyd's Rep 378

COMMONLY USED ACRONYMS AND ABBREVIATIONS

AGOA	*African Growth and Opportunity Act*
APP	*Appeal*
All N.L.R	*All Nigerian Law Reports*
BCA	*Bamenda Court of Appeal*
B2B	*Business to Business*
B2C	*Business to Consumers*
CC	*Code Civil*
CIV	*Civil*
CCLR	*Cameroon Common Law Report*
CASWP	*Court of Appeal, South West Province*
All ER	*All England Reports*
CISG	*United Nations Convention on Contracts for the International Sale of Goods*
CCJA	*Common Court of Justice and Arbitration*
CEMAC	*Communauté Economique et Monétaire de l'Afrique Centrale*
CO	*Company*
DEA	*Diplôme d'Etudes Approfondies*
Ed	*Edition*
HCSW	*High Court, South West*
NO	*Number*
UAGCL	*Uniform Act Relating to General Commercial Law*
UN	*United Nations*
UNIDROIT	*International Institute for the Unification of Private Laws*
OHADA	*Organisation pour l'Harmonisation en Afrique du Droit des Affaires*
UCC	*Uniform Commercial Code*

UA	*Uniform Act*
U.S.A.	*United States of America*
OAPI	*Organisation Africaine pour la Propriété Intellectuelle*
PARA	*Paragraph*
WIPO	*World Intellectual Property Organisation*
IP	*Intellectual Property*
IPR	*Intellectual Property Right*
NWLR	*Nigerian Weekly Law Reports*
No	*Number*
LTD	*Limited*
LGDJ	*Librairie General de Droit et de Jurisprudence*
K.B	*Kings Bench*
P.U.A	*Presses Universitaires d'Afrique*
P	*Page*
PP	*Pages*
SGA	*Sale of Goods Act*
Q.B.	*Queens Bench*
Vol.	*Volume*
V.	*Versus*

1

GENERAL INTRODUCTION

Background to the Study

In Sub-Saharan Africa generally, and Cameroon in particular, goods and services are bought and sold everywhere and at different prices. Some are expensive, some cheap and others moderate depending on the category, type of goods and the locality where they are found. Leaving the market force to determine the price ceiling and floor of goods and services in Cameroon will put consumers in an unfavourable angle. The issue of pricing has been a sensitive one in an economy all the time given that it has to do with money. This explains why there need to be a law regulating or governing commercial activities in general and pricing in particular. In effect, for the relationship between a supplier of goods and a retail seller, the "OHADA[1] Uniform Acts" are the business laws applicable in Cameroon and sixteen other West and Central African countries. For the relationship between a retail seller and a consumer, Cameroon's domestic consumer and contract laws apply.[2]To that effect, today in Cameroon there is Law No. 2015/018 of December 21 2015 governing commercial activity and despite the efforts put in place by

1 This French appellation refers to « Organisation pour L'Harmonisation en Afrique du Droit des Affaires ». The Treaty setting-up OHADA was signed at Port-Louis, Mauritius Island on 17 October 1993, as revised at Quebec, Canada, on 17 October 2008. The revisions became effective on 21 March 2010. As of July 7, 2010, the West African members of OHADA are Benin, Burkina Faso, Cote d'Ivoire, Guinea, Guinea-Bissau, Mali, Niger, Senegal, and Togo, and the Central African members of OAHDA are Central African Republic, Chad, Cameroon, Comoros, Congo, Equatorial Guinea, and Gabon. *See* http://<www.ohada.org > and http://<www.ohada.com>. On February 22, 2010, the Democratic Republic of Congo's president ratified the country's adoption of the OHADA treaty. By the treaty's terms, a country becomes a member sixty days after the note has been deposited in Senegal. OHADA Treaty, article52, paragraph 3.

2 Loi-Cadre 2011/012 du 6 mai 2011 portant protection du consommateur au Cameroun.

the Ministry of Trade and Commerce[3], there are still problems surrounding the pricing of goods and services in Cameroon. Retailers still retail goods above the retail price, some producers and manufacturers still sell goods at exorbitant prices when they move to the countryside.

Statement of the Problem

Business malpractices by sellers today include deception, false pretense, false promise, misrepresentation, concealment of facts which pose a great challenge to the law. Commercial buyers are increasingly the victim of a diverse and bewildering array of unscrupulous selling and deceptive business practices in a market overt.[4] By extension, this causes hardships to commercial buyers in their business relationship with consumers. In fact, these frauds undermine the consumer's confidence in the entire business community, thus injuring the goodwill of honest commercial buyers. Government has attempted isolated measures to contain these unfair practices but the degree of the practices largely outweighs these efforts.

Misrepresentation over the quality and prices of goods in the current market is a serious problem in a developing country like Cameroon. This is usually characterised by dishonesty of facts over the quality and prices of the goods being sold. The commercial buyer's problem, of course, is to identify quality. The presence of sellers in the local markets who are willing to offer inferior goods with low prices tends to drive the market of some specific brand of goods out of existence – as is the case of bad automobiles or building construction materials. It is this possibility that represents the major costs of dishonesty- for dishonest dealings tend to drive honest business dealings in some goods out of the market. There may be potential buyers of good quality products and there may be potential sellers of such products in the appropriate price range; however, the presence of dishonest sellers who wish to pawn bad wares as good wares tends to drive out the legitimate business, causing scarcity. The cost of dishonesty, therefore, lies not only in the amount by which the buyer is cheated; the cost also must include the loss incurred

[3] This Ministry was created by Decree No.88/204 of 5 February 1988, re-organising the Ministry of Commerce. This full text of this Ministerial Decree is found in *Juridis Périodique*, no. 5, 1991, p.13. This structure was created with the objective of protecting consumers and ensuring the technical supervision of the quality and quantity of goods through inspection.

[4] The market system in major cities in Cameroon which are publicly patronised at regular hours and acknowledged as markets qualify to be described as a market overt. However, it is generally admitted at common law that "market overt" is a legally constituted market, open on hours of sunrise and sunset and where goods for sale are openly displayed to any stand-by or passerby.

from reducing the size of the legitimate business of certain goods out of the market thereby affecting the country's economy.

A further exploration of the problem centres on the considerable evidence that quality variation is greater in underdeveloped than developed countries. Standardisation and quality control are still underdeveloped in most countries signatories to the OHADA treaty, such as Cameroon.[5] For instance, the need for quality control of export-import goods can be taken as one indicator for the influx of bad quality goods in the Cameroonian markets as an example. The importation rules in Cameroon like in other member States are not as efficient in ensuring the certification of goods into the country. There is still some laxity on the part of government institutions to strongly supervise the quality of goods in the markets. The magnitude of the problem of defective products may be better appreciated by bearing in mind the potential problem of product dumping from jurisdictions with stricter safety laws.[6] It is not inconceivable for unscrupulous foreign manufacturers to target the markets of developing countries with products that fail to meet the safety requirements of their home countries by charging low prices for those products in the developing countries. Products which have been banned or which had failed to get government approval in the developed countries are often dumped in developing countries.[7] Consequently, the local markets have been flooded with new products from different origins. This state of affairs is clearly evident with the proliferation of Chinese goods in the local markets.[8] This situation

5 Growth and Employment Strategy Paper; Refernce Framework fo Government Action over the period 2010–2020 for Cameroon.

6 Samgena D. Galega,"Strict Liability for Defective Products in Cameroon? Some Illuminating Lessons from Abroad", (2004) 48 (2) *Journal of African Law*, pp. 239–270, p.253,254.

7 This is common with vendors in an open market in most Cameroonian cities, who are by the side of the roads, peddling medicines, pharmaceutical products, and many other kinds of produce, including telephone sets and household utensils. Almost certainly in the informal sector of the Cameroonian economy are the shopkeepers who, from the stalls that line the streets, sell second-used clothes, hand'made furnitures, small electonic equipments from abroad. Also included is the caterer or tailor whose business is in the formal sector but who, who from the back room hidden from tax collector and government agents from the Ministry of Trade and Commerce, run a dress shop or sell electronic items already used from abroad to sell to trusted customers. All these nano-entrepreneurs deliberately run away from formal government authority because as one principal reason, due to the defective state of the goods they sell and the absence of business license. See Claire Moore Dickerson,"Informal-Sector Entrepreneurs, Development and Formal Law: A Functional Understanding of Business Law", (2011) 59 *American Journal of Comparative Law*, pp.159–226, p. 180.

8 It is commonplace to find a high incidence of Chinese goods in shops and streets of most towns. Preference of these goods by commercial buyers is because of their cheap prices and easy affordability. However, the local consumers continue to complain about the poor quality of these goods in terms of durability. Such goods include from clothings, shoes electronics and electrical equipments.

has some significant consequences on the purchasing public because these imported goods fail to meet the expected standards of buyers due to the laxity of the government in ensuring the quality control of those products.

It is alarming that in most markets today there is rampant fraud in the selling business of some commodities. The feature of the tort of passing-off[9] is commonplace in some markets of some Cameroonian big cities. There has been a rampant illegal activity that consists of filling up empty containers of products (perfumes and other cosmetics and liquor bottles) with deficiencies in quantity supplied to reselling buyers. Government has attempted isolated measures to contain these unfair practices but the degree of the practices largely outweighs the efforts.

The proliferation of these issues today is an indication that Cameroon still has a problem with her quality control of goods pricing policy and thus there is the need to redress it legally. It could be that the laws are good but implementation is weak due to the fact that some of the administrators working with this Ministry of Trade do not have adequate experience on commerce. Again, it could be that the manufacturers, wholesalers and retailers are unnecessarily stubborn and the reason why 'black market' is a normal practice in Cameroon.

Research Questions

Flowing from the problem are the main and specific questions:

Main Research Question:

How effective are the laws in place in guaranteeing the quality and adequate prices of goods in the Cameroonian economy?

Specific Questions:

The following specific questions were formulated to guide the conduct of this research:

- What is the concept of pricing?

[9] This is an economic tort, which relates to the selling of goods under such a name, mark, description or otherwise in such a manner as to mislead the public into believing that the goods or merchandise belongs to another person.

- Do the laws adequately guarantee the quality of goods sold by the seller?
- How effective is the control of prices of goods?
- What are the offences and sanctions on illegal and unlawful pricing of goods?
- What are the remedies available to the buyer for the seller's liability for the non-conformity of goods to the contract of sale?

Hypothesis

This thesis has main and sub- hypotheses:

Main Hypothesis:

This work is based on the assumption that although some legal measures or requirements have been put in place to afford protection to buyers of goods, those safeguards seem not to be adequately implemented in assuring the quality and adequate pricing of goods supplied in the markets.

Sub-Hypotheses

- ► HO 1: The laws do not adequately guarantee the quality of the goods by the seller.
- ► HO 2: The control of the prices of goods is not effective.
- ► HO 3: Formal law provides sanctions to illegal and unlawful pricing of goods.
- ► HO 4: Formal law provides remedies which can avail a in the event of the seller's non-conformity of quality of goods.

Research Objectives

This book has general and specific objectives:

General Objective

The general objective of this study is to examine the effectiveness of the laws in ensuring conformity of the quality and prices of goods under a contract of sale.

Specific Objectives

- To achieve this broad objective set out above, the study will look at the following specific objectives:
- To clearly articulate the meaning of pricing.
- To carefully examine the provisions of the laws governing the seller's duty of conformity of quality of goods.
- To clearly assess the effectiveness of the control of prices of goods.
- To highlight the offence and sanctions on illegal and unlawful pricing of goods.
- To examine remedies available to buyers.
- To achieve these objectives, this article adopts a critical and analytical approach in interpreting the provisions of the legal instruments regulating pricing system of goods as applicable in Cameroon. Emphasis will deeply dwell on contract of sale of goods[10] than on contract of services.

Research Methodology

This research invariably adopts the legal empirical research method, which is better adapted to address the salient legal issues raised. This research essentially used a content analysis of both primary and secondary materials in the relevant domain. The research adopts a critical and analytical approach in interpreting the provisions of the OHADA Uniform Act on General Commercial Law, and of national and international instruments regulating the sale of goods contracts.

This work embarked on the collection and analysis of primary data in the form of statutes, decided cases from the local courts, decisions of the Common Court of Justice and Arbitration in Abidjan and the Supreme Court in England, as well as foreign cases touching on issues of sale of goods.

In addition, extensive was made of secondary sources of literature on the subject. The researchers used content analysis of journals, periodicals, textbooks, conference proceedings and policy documents relevant to this work, which were found in the libraries of the Universities of Buea, Dschang, Douala and Yaoundé II – Soa in Cameroon.

10 As governed by Article 3 paragraph 1 of the 2015 Law and Article 234 paragraph 1 of the Uniform Act.

The researcher conducted systematic interviews with businessmen in the market cities of Bamenda, Douala and Yaoundé, and consumer associations, legal practitioners, and government officials engaged with the regulation of commercial activities within the country. This gives first hand impression about their perception of problems inherent in the business relationship with sellers and buyers. The responses from the unstructured interviews constitute one of the primary sources of materials for the work. The interviews were effected in English or French depending on the interviewee's preferences.

Conceptual and Theoretical Framework

This section shall in the main dwell on the core concepts and theories which underpin this research.

Freedom of Contract Theory

The classical theory of contract is based on the idea of freedom of contract which was an offspring of the *laissez-faire* economic theory championed by Adam Smith. Hence, the will of the contracting parties become the source of their mutual rights and duties which the contracting parties hold with respect to one another. The essential teaching in this respect and in connection to this research study is the principle of economic freedom under a contract of sale of goods. According to Adam Smith[11], everyone has the economic freedom to act on his or her self-interest in order to achieve his economic desires. Consequently, in their relentless effort to achieve this economic desire, they are guided by an invisible hand, which ensures that while seeking to promote their self-interest, they incidentally promote the public interest as well although they did not set out to do so.[12]

Certainly, there is a paternalistic ground for legal rules to regulate and protect the very interest of the contracting parties as well as the consuming public at large.[13] This concept of legal paternalism is instrumental to this thesis in that under a contract of sale, the seller's duty of conformity is embodied in a magnitude of implied rules contained in articles 255 *et seq.*

---

11 *Wealth of Nations,* (Vol.1, Dent 1910) p. 421

12 S. Todd Lowry, "Bargain and Contract Theory in Law and Economics", (1976) 10 (1) *Journal of Economic Issues*, pp.1–22, p. 13.

13 Michael J. Trebilock, *The Limits of Freedom of Contract* (Havard University Press, 1993) pp. 149–151.

of the Uniform Act on General Commercial Law to ascertain the quality of goods to the commercial buyer.

This book seeks to argue that the freedom of traders of goods to enter into a contract of sale for the supply of quality goods in conformity with the contract terms in the market is much dictated too by the demands of consumers in insisting for quality goods. Hence, in spite of the freedom of the parties in their contract of sale, such measures under the OHADA Uniform Act by extension, tend to be protective to consumers, (who are the end-users of those goods), and the economy of the state. Arguably, this research is working on the premise that the idea of freedom of contract is today a pretty sick horse, because of socio-legal and economic considerations among the economic actors. This relates to the fact that the expansive duties imposed on the seller in satisfying the preferences of the commercial buyer under their business contract, are also by analogy serve as measures to protect the development of a country by requiring sellers to do legitimate business with commercial buyers.

Interest Theory

Exponents of the interest theory, such as Ihering and Bentham[14] argued in favour of the idea that individuals have interests which frequently conflict. This theory demonstrates that a claim-right is an interest protected by a duty. To identify the person to whom I owe my duty (the holder of the correlative claim-right), we need to work out whose interest is protected by my duty. The interest theorists happily concede that when duties do not protect individual interest, they are regarded as protecting collective interests. Hence, interest theorists regard the correlativity of claim-rights and duties as strict and universal: for them, all claim-rights entail duties, and all duties entail claim-rights.

This theory is central to this thesis in that the expansive seller's duties to supply goods in conformity with the terms of the contract of sale as contained in article 255 of the Uniform Act on General Commercial Law stand as a fact to protect the interest of commercial buyers of goods. The breach of these duties by the seller to provide conforming goods is an injury to the interests of commercial buyers and entitles the latter to claim remedies. Hence, the seller's duty is correlative to the commercial buyer's claim-right to damages

[14] N.E. Simmonds, *Central Issues in Jurispudence, Justice, Law and Rights* (2nd edition, Sweet & Maxwell, London) 2002, pp.304–307.

in so far there is evidence that the seller has failed in its contractual duty of conformance.

Economic Theoretical Perspective

Two kinds of theories are going to be examined here: the theory of price and marginal utility and the information theory and welfare perspectives.

The Theory of Price and Marginal Utility

The needs and wants of buyers remain at the centre of our economic system. An individual decides freely on how to spend his or her income. The concept of money naturally proceeds from the idea that the recipient has the right to choose what he or she will buy with it from the range of goods and services which are available to the buyer and the restrictions on the individual's freedom of choice are less obvious than they may be in other respects.[15]

In a contract of sale of goods, the issue of price largely determines the quality of goods in the market. Similarly, the commercial buyer would achieve that objective by adjusting his income for each goods or service in accordance with the price of the goods offered by the seller. The utility of the goods to the commercial buyer is for resale and thus, the price is of consequence to his business and customers. Inevitably, if local consumers are unable to freely bargain because of high prices of goods in the marketplace, the demand is likely to be virtually insatiable for the commercial buyer and other non-market methods must therefore be used in deciding who is to buy them. The philosophy behind this action is based on Jeremy Bentham's jurisprudence on utilitarianism, which advocates for the "welfare" of individuals.[16] His argument is constructed from the viewpoint of rational interest which explains that every person would prefer a set of rules that advances its preferences at the expense of everyone; but the best it can hope for is a set of rules that serves the aggregate welfare.

There is an economic view that just as producers want to earn maximum profit in the same way the seller or buyer equally wants to gain maximum from the goods which he buys as per the price in order to derive maximum

---

15 *Ibid*, p. 324.

16 N.E. Simmonds, *Central Issues in Jurispudence, Justice, Law and Rights*, *Op cit.*, p.19.

satisfaction from the money he spends.[17] Therefore, the pattern of money expenditure varies with the range of goods and their prices in the market. The individual buying these goods expect them to be of satisfactory quality and be useful to him. In effect, price control of certain goods must be checked, should be the concern of the government in curtailing the excessive freedom of businessmen in the augmentation of prices of goods.

Information Theory and Welfare Perspective

This research deals with the issues addressed both from the information asymmetries and the welfare perspective. The information theory or signal theory relates to product warranty policy. It emphasises warranty terms which provide information to users of goods about the merchantability of the commodity in the market. This theory regards the 'market' for information about products.[18] Manufacturers or producers are required under this theory to draft warranties in simple and readily understood language in order to reduce the difficulty of comprehending warranty content. It also requires the disclosure of all important provisions conspicuously and to display warranties prominently so that they are available for buyer inspection prior to purchase of the product. Under this theory it is rather costly for the buyer to determine precisely product reliability at the time of purchasing through direct inspection. A buyer may view warranty as a 'signal' of product reliability which to some extent is related negatively with the cost of warranty coverage.

Though this theory is advanced to deal specifically with consumer product warranty, it is also of interest to professional traders under a contract of sale in the light of the principle of policy and the law. This is because the responsibility for defective goods rests upon the seller who is the person who distributed the goods to the public. The commercial buyer cares because he will be selling those products to the retail buyer. Circumstances may arise where the seller or commercial buyer buys with an intention of further processing or fabricating the goods or seller may also be a producer or manufacturer of goods sold to the retail buyer. In this situation, the latter needs to be informed on the warranty content of the goods available to him for inspection prior to delivery for the interest of his business. Therefore, on the basis of this, the commercial buyer is entitled to protection of his interest

[17] In conventional supply and demand analysis, it is assumed that in most contexts more goods or services will be supplied at higher than lower prices and that fewer goods or services will demand at higher prices than lower prices.

[18] G. J. Stigler, "The Economics of Information", (1961) 69 *Journal of Political Economy*, p.213.

within the scope of seller's responsibilities.[19]

In the welfare perspective model, it is supported by Paretian welfare justifications for private exchanges.[20] The organising assumption of this model is that one party to a contract is substantially less well informed about some aspect of the contract subject-matter than the other party. The Paretian justification further argues that both parties to an exchange are rendered better off by it – in terms of the subjectively perceived impact of the exchange on their respective utility functions – or they would not have entered into it. But if at least one party inaccurately perceives or evaluates the impact of the exchange on her utility, we can no longer be confident that the exchange will in fact render both parties better off. Proceeding from this argument, the author contends that to encourage appropriate circumspection on the part of sellers in claims they make about goods they are selling whose histories they are not fully informed of, the law would be justified in providing the buyer with relief. Such a conduct on the part of the sellers in their transaction induced by fraudulent representation of the goods they sell is unlikely to discourage buyers generally in the long – run to buy goods.

Human Rights and Ethical Theories

Legal and Rights Perspective

Commercial buyers as well as consumers have the right to make an informed choice over the kind of goods they buy or consume. This issue raises legal and ethical questions. The legal basis for this relates to the fact that it is an inalienable human right for any ordinary commercial buyer or consumer to make an informed judgment of what he chooses to buy. To a commercial buyer, this right is important to the resaleability of the goods as this is what he expects under his contract of sale with the seller with a view to satisfying the demands or needs of his customers. The commercial buyer cares because he does not want to be saddled with a product which may injure the health, religion and life of his customers. Article 25 (1) of the 1948 Universal Declaration of Human Rights[21] provides *inter alia* that:

---

19 Robert C. Brown, "The Liability of Retail Policies for Defective Food Products", (1939) 23 *Minnesota Law Review*, pp. 585–611, p.585.

20 Michael J. Trebilock, *The Limits of Freedom of Contract*, *op cit.*, pp.103–110.

21 The United Nations 1948 Universal Declaration of Human Rights, available at <http:#www.hrweb.org/legal/udhr.html> (last accessed on 27 April 2010).

> *everyone has the right to a standard of living adequate for the health and wellbeing of himself and of his family including food....Arguably, inherent in the right to food is the right to choose which food to eat.*

As a matter of fact, individuals might wish to know whether the food they buy has been genetically modified (GM) with animal contents either because they are vegetarians or for religious reasons. They could justify their demands to know and make appropriate choice by virtue of the provisions of Articles 1(1) and 18 (1), (2) and (3) of the United Nations International Covenant on Civil and Political Rights.[22] While examining the role of the consumer in GM food regulation, it is argued that no GM regulation is complete if visibility is not given to the consumer's right to know the GM components of their food, even if such food had passed public health or environmental safety muster.[23] This argument is premised on the proposition that consumer empowerment in this respect is as much a human right as an ethical or moral imperative. The central argument is that the consumer should be empowered through the labelling of products. From this standpoint, commercial buyers of goods are under the duty to have knowledge of the type of products that is free from any defect in its packaging and labelling in order to satisfy their customer's demands.

Additionally, most countries have constitutional and legal provisions guaranteeing the consuming public's right of choice directly or indirectly. For instance, the Cameroon Constitution[24] in its preamble adheres to the development, use, enjoyment and disposal of goods by every individual. It could be agreed that it is on the basis of this that the consumers in Cameroon keep on pressing the commercial buyers to provide them with quality goods in order to make informed choices in the markets.

Ethical Perspectives

The right to know and make informed purchase decisions also has ethical implications. One of the ethical theories used to assess quality of goods is the ethical theory of "consequentialism", which is also founded on moral theory. An individual is morally required to perform a particular action or

22 Article 1(1) of this Covenant provides that "all people have the right of self-determination". By virtue of that right they freely determine their political status and freely pursue their economic, social and cultural development. This is available at < http:#www.hrweb.org/legal/cpr.html> Article % 2017.2 (last accessed on April 2010)

23 Taiwo A. Oriola,"Consumer Dilemmas:The Right to Know, Safety, Ethics and Policy of Genetically Modified Food",(2002) *Singapore Journal of Legal Studies*, pp. 514–573, p.522.

24 Law No. 96–06 of 18 January 1996 to amend the Constitution of 2 June 1972, available at <http://confinder.richmond.edu:admin:docs:cameroon.pdf> (downloaded on October 19, 2010).

do a certain specific thing only if it would result in a greater good and benefit to the world than if he had chosen to perform one of the alternative actions.[25] How do we assess if genetically modified food labelling policy, for example, would be more beneficial or lead to the greater good of the society than non-genetically modified food labelling policy and *vice versa*? The easiest way to do this would be through a consensus, and let the people decide which would be more beneficial: a labelling or non-labelling policy?

Viewed from the foregoing perspective, it would be morally wrong and unethical to make definitive business rule regarding price or labelling or packaging without consulting the stakeholders whom the decision was supposed to benefit.

Significance of the Study

The importance of this study cannot be over emphasised. It touches on a socio-legal and economic issues which are very topical in the business world. Sellers and commercial buyers are at daggers-drawn over the raison d'être of enhancing ethical behaviour in business transactions. The business world is moving now from *caveat emptor* to *caveat venditor.*

This study will be quite edifying to law students with interests in the OHADA Sales Law, merchants, legal practitioners, sociologists, as it will contribute to the existing legal literature in this area of the law, thus stimulating thoughts for a way forward in the quest to bring more clarifications for law reform. The research will establish equality and certainty in the business of sale of goods.

This research suggests and develops new approaches to the provisions of the OHADA Uniform Act on General Commercial Law as it focuses more on the relationship between the seller and the commercial buyer in an effort to appreciate the impact that the OHADA Uniform Act on General Commercial Law may have on the protection of consumers in Cameroon. The work also adequately highlights domestic laws governing commercial activity and consumer protection in Cameroon. The work will go a long way to raise the awareness of consumers and will obviously advocate for the application of the draft Uniform Act on Consumer Law. This work will definitely contributes to the understanding of the provisions of the OHADA Uniform Act on General Commercial Law.

---

25 See Robert Streiffer, *"Ethical Behaviour in Modern Biology"*, Course Overview for 2001 at the Department of Philosophy, University of Wisconsin-Madison, available at < http:#www.bitech-info.net/biothics_corse.html> (last accessed in June 2009).

Justification of the Research

Research on the quality control of goods and pricing is timely. It is justified for addressing the pertinent issues of buyers' dissatisfaction over the poor quality of goods and discriminatory prices in the market. It comes at a time when consumers are vulnerable to such business malpractices orchestrated by unscrupulous sellers in the local markets.

Furthermore, this research will go a long way in raising the awareness of sellers and producers of goods within the OHADA territories. In fact, it reiterates the principle of '*caveat venditor*' (let the seller beware) because it argues that the seller can also be deceived in a market transaction with producers. Eventually, the seller is bound to take responsibility for the products he sells that are not in conformity with the specifications of the contract of sale as required by the commercial buyer.

2

THE MEANING OF THE CONCEPT OF PRICING POLICY

Introduction

Policy here, first of all is a plan of action, statement of aims and ideals, especially one made by a government, business company or individual. Price on its own part is the sum of money for which something is sold or bought. Reconciling these two definitions, pricing policy in Cameroon will mean the plan of action or ideals made by the government of Cameroon to ensure that goods and services are bought and sold within a rate favourable to citizens. This explains why the 2015 Law[26] governing commercial activity in Cameroon holds that the prices of goods and rates of services shall be freely determined through healthy and fair market competition. However, the determination of the prices and rates of some sensitive products and services, particularly basic necessities or monopolies, may be subject to the prior approval procedure, according to the conditions and procedures laid down by regulation. The list of goods and services whose prices and rates are subject to the prior approval procedure shall be prepared by order of the Minister in charge of prices, who here is the Minister of Trade in Cameroon.

Decisions relating to the prices and rate of some products and services shall be made by an Order of the Minister of Trade who may delegate authority to Regional Governors or approved public bodies. It is worthy to say here that the prices and rates of some products and services may also be fixed through consultation between the Minister of Trade and various businessmen conducting a business in different sectors of the economy. The memorandum of understanding resulting from such consultations shall be binding by order of the Minister of Trade. Any sale of goods or provision of

[26] Section 44.

service that does not fall under free pricing shall be done in compliance with regulated, approved or coordinated prices, as the case may be, in accordance with the regulations in force.[27]

Most well managed manufacturing enterprises have a clear cut advertising policy, product customer policy and distribution-channel policy. But pricing decision remains a patchwork of ad hoc decisions. In many, otherwise well managed firms, price policy have been dealt with on a crisis basis. This kind of price management discourages the kind of systematic analysis needed for clear cut pricing policies. In Cameroon, products and services have been categorized into three main heads; there are goods with homologated prices[28], goods whose prices are made or fixed after consultation between the Minister of Trade and various businessmen. The last category of goods is those bought and sold under the free pricing mechanism. At this point, it would be necessary to understand the meaning of price.

The Legal Conception of Price

Arguably, the issue of price cannot be discussed in isolation from a contract of sale of goods which is the very context it operates.

The contract of sale of goods, defined

Contract of sale of goods is by far the most common type of contracts and often concern goods of a utilitarian nature, with a clearly defined purpose. People enter into agreements every day to buy goods for a variety of reasons. The most obvious, of course, is to enjoy and acquire their ownership and use them for different purposes. Most, if not all, contracts, whether they involve goods, real property or services, are necessarily economic activities. This is *a fortiori* true of the types of contracts which are the subject of this study: contract of sale of manufactured goods purchased for resale. Importantly, the utility of these types of goods for the buyer may be influenced by a broad range of factors. The buyer may choose particular goods based on their brand or reputation. The environmental and social practices involved in their manufacture may also be significant. Moreover, consumer tastes and preferences matter to the commercial buyer, as the brand of goods in the markets may rise and fall.

[27] Section 45 of the 2015 Law governing Commercial Activity in Cameroon.

[28] Cement, Sugar, Zinc, Iron Rode, Gas, Petrol etc.

As a general principle, the law relating to a contract of sale is an aspect of the general law of contract. A contract of sale is first and foremost a contract, that is, a binding consensual transaction based on agreement to buy and an agreement to sell.[29] It appears therefore that it cannot be examined in isolation from its very context.

The Uniform Act does not expressly define what constitutes a 'contract of sale.' However, it can be established indirectly from the provisions of the Act setting out the duties of the seller[30] and of the buyer.[31] According to those provisions, the contract of sale is a contract by which one party (seller) is obliged to deliver the goods, and to transfer property on the goods, to the other party (buyer) at an agreed price.[32] This denotes the fact that a sales contract is a reciprocal exchange of goods which one party binds itself to transfer against the price. This is a clear confirmation found under Article 250 para.1 UAGCL; the main obligations of the seller are to deliver the goods, hand over any documents relating to the goods. Under Article 262 UAGCL, the main obligations of the buyer are to pay the price and take delivery of the goods.

For more clarification, a contract of sale is defined in Section 2 of the Sale of Goods Act as:

> *...a contract by which the seller transfers or agrees to transfer property in goods to the buyer for money consideration, called the price.*

Also, in the French Civil code, a sales contract is merely between two parties, one party who is under the obligation to deliver the contract goods and the other one who is under the obligation to pay the price.[33]

To be concise, we can state the general proposition that the Uniform Act follows the positions at Common Law and the Civil code, by holding that for sales contract to exist, the goods, must be definite that is, must exist, be movable, be capable of being determined,[34] and legal.[35] At Common Law these requirements are also observed.

The root definition in the above definitions contains a number of ingredients, which are pointers in perceiving the essential requirements and nature of a sales contract.

29 Atiyah et al., *The Sale of Goods*, 12th Edition, Longman, Pitman Publishing, London, 2010, p.6.
30 Article 250 (Conforming goods)
31 Article 262 (to purchase)
32 *Ibid.* (refers to buyer's obligation to pay the price)
33 "La vente est une convention par laquelle l'un s'oblige à livrer une chose, et l'autre à la payer" : See Civil Codes (CC) of Cameroon, Article 1582 CC; Côte d'Ivoire, Article 1582 CC; France, Article 1582 CC.
34 Cameroon, Article 1129 CC; Côte d'Ivoire, Article 1129 CC.
35 Cameroon, Article 1128 CC; Côte d'Ivoire, Article 1128 CC.

We are concerned here with the principal duty of the seller to deliver goods of conformity under a contract of sale as formulated under the UAGCL, the heart of the seller's contract obligation[36] of conformity. Therefore, to identify the ambit of 'conformity', it is relevant to identify the 'goods' that are the object of the OHADA Uniform Act on General Commercial Law which warrants the payment of a price by the commercial buyer.

For parties to have a legal contract, some requirements are indispensable. Among others is consideration which is manifested through the payment of a price.

But before that is imposed on the seller, there must be an agreement between the buyer and the seller in order to establish a contractual commercial relationship. Contract formation[37] is an important aspect as far as contract for a sale of goods is concerned. This is because it is at this level that parties freely express themselves on how their transaction should look like be it at the regional or global levels. Another pertinent issue is that there has to be a valid and legally enforceable agreement for a sale to be envisaged. What makes such enforceability in addition to the elements of a contract are mutual assent though the test usually to be applied is not what each party in fact had in mind but what each ought reasonably to have assumed from the language and conduct of the other,[38] the legal capacity[39] of the parties, intention to be legally bound,[40]

---

[36] This duty is governed by Article 255 para.1 UAGCL. See also, Larry Dimatteo et al., "The Interpretive Turn in International Sales Law: An Analysis of Fifteen Years of CISG Jurisprudence", (2004) 24 *Northwestern Journal of International Law and Business*, pp.299–392, p. 292, commenting on Article 35 CISG which also spells out the seller's duties.

[37] Etienne Nsie, " La Formation de la Vente Commerciale en Afrique" (1999) 829 *Penant*, p 5.

[38] *Smith v. Hughes* (1871) LR 6 QB 597; *Reardon Smith Ltd v. Hansen-Tangen* [1976] 3 ALL ER 570; *The Hannah Blumenthal* [1983] 1 ALL ER 34; *The Leonidas D* [1983] 3 ALL ER 737. This is otherwise where one party's understanding of the contract was known to the other, even though not matching his own (*Hartog v. Colin and Shields* [1939] 3 ALL ER 566.

[39] See now Minors' Contract Act 1987, which repealed the Infants Relief Act 1874, leaving the enforceability of contracts entered into by minors to be governed exclusively by common law rules and by the provisions of the 1987 Act relating to ratification. See G. H. Treitel, *Law of Contract* (11th edition , Sweet & Maxwell, London 2003), ch 13; Cheshire, Fifoot and Furmston, *Law of Contract* (14thedition, Butterworths, 2001), ch13.

[40] There are certain situations in which people find it convenient to fudge the question whether a legal commitment is intended, in order to be able to do the deal. The typical case is the so-called letter of comfort, which may or not generate a contract, depending upon the intentions of the partiesas determined in the terms of the contract of comfort. Inevitably, agreement is bought at the price of uncertainty. See. For example, *Kleinwort Benson Ltd v. Malaysia Mining Corp Bhd*[1989] 1 ALL ER 785 (letter of comfort held not to be contractual); and, for a similar finding in relation to a letter of intent, *British Steel Corp v. Claveland Bridge and Engineering Co Ltd* [1984] 1 ALL ER 504. By contrast, in *Wilson Smitheett& Cape (Sugar) Ltd v. Bangladesh Sugar & Food Industries Corp.* [1986] 1 Lloyd's Rep 378, the letter of intent was held to be contractual.

consideration[41] and the form[42] of the contract.

In order to have an understanding of facts in which these complex transactions occur, it is appropriate to address the issue of consideration (which represents the price) necessary for the effective conclusion of a sales contract. It is of interest to look at what the OHADA Uniform At on General Commercial Law[43] (UAGCL) provides as to the conclusion of a sale contract. It is also important to point out that some elements are not expressed in the Uniform Act but are indirectly stipulated.

Consideration

The UAGCL does not expressly define consideration. But, it is deduced from the duties of the parties. The seller agrees to transfer goods to the buyer who in return pays for them in a monetary form known as price. The buyer is further expected to take all necessary steps for the effective payment of the price.[44] Under the Uniform Act, a contract of sale cannot be concluded without the specification of price.

The doctrine of consideration is peculiar to the Common law system. Generally, consideration is something of value in the eyes of the law. It follows that a valuable consideration can be some right, interest, profit or benefit accruing to one party or some forbearance, detriment, loss or responsibility, given, suffered or undertaken by the other.[45] Whether through doctrine or case law, the appropriate definition of consideration seems to lay emphasis on the value of what is exchanged between the parties.[46] At Common law, it does not matter whether the value is too small or too high. What matters is the mere value of the consideration, no matter how small it is, as it was held in *Thomas v. Thomas*[47]when analysing the adequacy of the consideration.[48]

Consideration can also be described differently in sale of goods, for

---

41 See Paul Mitchell and John Phillips, "Contractual Nexus: Is Reliance Essential?"(2002) 22(1) *OJLS* 115.

42 Statute of Fraud 1677, section4.

43 Hereinafter referred variously as 'UAGCL' or 'Uniform Act'. This is known in French as OHADA, *Acte Uniforme portant sur le Droit Commercial Général*, found in the Official Gazette of OHADA, No. 23, of 15th February 2011. It is also available *at* http://www.ohada.com/textes.

44 Article 264 UAGCL.

45 *Currie v. Misa* (1975) LR 10 Exch 153, 162).

46 Hugh Beale et al., *Cases, Materials and Text on Contract Law,*(Hart Publishing, 2002) p.141.

47 (1842) 2 QB 851

48 Michael Furmston, *Law of Contract, Law of Contract,* (14thedition, Butterworths, 2001), p. 106; Nicholas B, *The French Law of Contract, op cit,* p.113.

instance, as the price of the promise, as it was held in the case of *Dunlop Pneumatic Tyre Co. v. Selfridge Ltd.*[49] In such case, the House of Lords decided that a promise can be enforceable if it is bought for a price required; consideration here was the price.

In practice, the doctrine of consideration is divided into two categories: Executory and Executed consideration. In a sale of goods transaction, it will be described as "executory" when a promise is made in return of a counter promise and it will be executed when made against the performance of an act.[50]

While executed and "executory" considerations are valid considerations, common law treats past consideration as an absence of consideration. In *Re McArdle*,[51] the promise was not binding on children and the consideration was past. The Court of Appeal in this decision took in consideration that the children promised to repay the expenses of the plaintiff after the work was completed.

Under Civil law, where a contract arises from an agreement, it is understood to be as a result of the consensus of the minds of the contracting parties, Common law departs from a promise supported by consideration.[52] Therefore, consideration at this stage appears to be relevant because a promise is not a contract unless converted into an agreement upon acceptance.[53] The promises lead then the parties to bargain. This might be the reason why consideration might be considered a consensus of intentions, a consensus of two promises. In a comparative perspective, with regard to onerous French contracts for instance, a promise amounting to consideration may fall within the criteria of "*la cause*". Thus, in a sales contract situation, the buyer's obligation to pay for the price will be treated as follows; the consideration supporting the contract and "*la cause*" of the seller's obligation to transfer the property of the goods. Consequently, in a sales contract, the *cause* of the seller remains the delivery of the goods and that of the buyer, why he wants the goods.[54] Based on this example, in a substantive note, what may amount to consideration under English Law, will likely be regarded as cause under French civil law.

In the case of the formation of the contract of sale of goods under English law, the consideration consists of rendering of mutual promise and most

49 [1915] A.C 847 p 855.
50 Michael Furmston, *Law of Contract, op cit*, p .97.
51 [1951] Ch. 669.
52 Nicholas B., *The French Law of Contract,* Butterworths,London, 1982,pp. 39–65;
53 *Carlill v. Carbolic Smoke Ball co (1893) 1 QB 257, AC.*
54 Henri &Leon Mazeaud et al.,*Obligations, théorie générale,Leçons De Droit Civil,*(9 ed., Montchrestien,1998) p.271–272.

importantly the payment of the price. Only promises supported by a legal consideration (price) are legally binding. Generally speaking, the central function of the doctrine of consideration is to prevent people from making gratuitous promises, and the purpose of the law of consideration is to distinguish between gratuitous and non-gratuitous promises. The price is money which has to be paid for the purchase of something.

Just as the CISG,[55] the issue of price under the UAGCL can be inferred from the mutual exchanges of goods on the one hand for price on the other. Article 263 of the Uniform Act stipulates that:

> *A sale may not be validly concluded without a specification of the price in the contract of sale, unless the parties referred to the price generally charged at the time of conclusion of the contract in the commercial sector considered for the same goods sold under similar circumstances.*

The wording of the above article shows that price is a determining factor in the formation of a contract of sale. It represents a consideration on the part of the seller while transfer of title is for the buyer. There is however, the possibility for concluding contracts without specifying the price by making reference to the price generally charged at the time of the contract.[56] From the consumer's point of view, price is usually defined "as what the consumer must give up to purchase a product or service".[57] Even though the parties in their contract are free to debate on the price of the object to be sold, they are prices of certain commodities which have been statutorily fixed by the government, at times in, relation to the trade usage and practice. In practice, sellers usually have discriminatory prices of goods they sell at their marketplaces. The prices of some goods do not represent the real value of such goods, a situation which may put commercial buyers into difficulties vis-à-vis their customers in particular. However, through the enactment of price control legislation, sellers of certain commodities are under a statutory duty to respect price arrangement. In this regard, a seller has a duty to deliver goods in conformity with the price imposed by the government.

---

55 Article 55 CISG.

56 Edie Diable Pascal, Contract of Sale of Goods under the OHADA Uniform Act on General Commercial Law, The Common Law and the CISG: A Comparative Study, (Masters Dissertation, Faculty of Law and Political Science, University of Dschang, 2011) p.45.

57 J. Paul Peter & Jerry C. Olson, Consumer Behavior and Marketing Strategy, (2nd edition, Homewood 1998) pp. 496–510.

The Categorisation of a Contract of Sale under the Uniform Act

The categorisation of a contract of sale under the OHADA Uniform Act on General Commercial Law is very restrictive. The preoccupation of the Act relates to contracts for the acquisition of goods for business purposes which can be identified as B2B contracts.B2B contracts refer to sales contracts between two professional sellers. It is often referred to as "business to business contract". On the other hand, business to consumer sales (B2C) contracts refer to sales contracts concluded between a professional seller and a consumer. The UAGCL does not cover B2C contracts but the expected outcome of a B2B contract under the UAGCL is to proceed to a B2C contract. In fact, the goods involved in a B2B transaction are the subject in a B2C contract. Consumers are the end-users of those goods.

Generally, the distinction B2B and B2C in sales contract is often found in civil law countries, whereas such a distinction does not exist at Common law.

Business to Business

Today, the Uniform Act is the applicable law in the OHADA Member States with regard to the B2B contract.[58] Under the Uniform Act, a B2B contract is conducted by a trader (*commerçant*).[59]

Generally, in order to determine whether a person or an entity is a trader, it is important to find out whether it carries out a particular transaction on a regular basis. Traders are considered to be those who engage in commerce as their usual professional activities.[60] Thus, traders in this sense could be anyone, a human being, a legal person including all commercial companies, or a person governed by public law.[61] As concerns contracts of sale of goods, the Uniform Act has provided rules for natural persons and corporations who may exercise such sales contract.[62]

58 These contracts are regulated by all the Articles which fall under Book IV of the UAGCL.

59 Athanase Foko, Le Statut du Commerçant dans l'espace OHADA, (P.U.A., Collection Vade-Mecum, Yaoundé, 2005) p.19–20; Jean-Marie Nyama, Eléments de Droit des Affaires Cameroun-OHADA, (Presse de l'UCAC, Collection Apprendre, Yaoundé2002) p.18–19.

60 Article 2 UAGCL. The language in this text is ambiguous to a Common law reader.

61 Article 1 Uniform Act. To a Common law lawyer, this notion seems strange since it has no specific legal connotation in the Common law system. A close idea to this in view to ease understanding may relate to public sector of the economy, that is public enterprises. Many public bodies are corporations in a similar sense to private companies operating in a private sector. Therefore, a public body is an organisation set up in the public interest to carry out a public service function. It may be a public enterprise of an administrative or commercial kind. They have an inherent power to protect the public interest.

62 Book IV UAGCL.

However, it would not be necessary here to elaborate on the broad categories of legal persons that may be involved in commercial activity under the Uniform Act on General Commercial Law.

Under the UAGCL, the seller and the buyer must be traders. In fact, the Uniform Act restricts the status of the parties that may be party to a contract of sale. The status of the traders, either a physical person[63] or a company,[64] must be acquired by registration in the Commercial Registry.[65]

The Uniform Act has listed out the different types of business transactions it intends to cover. These transactions include; the purchase of movable or immovable property for resale; banking, stock-exchange, currency exchange, brokerage, insurance, and transit transactions; contracts between traders for business purposes; the industrial exploitation of mines, quarries and any natural resource deposit and rental of movable property; manufacturing, transportation and telecommunication operations; the operations of trade middlemen such as commission, brokerage and agency, as well as middleman's operations relating to the purchase, underwriting, sale or rental of immovable property, businesses, shares in commercial companies or property development companies; a bill of exchange, a promissory note, and a warrant.[66] The list is not exhaustive.

The type of B2B contract with which we are concerned here is a contract between traders for business purposes what is here referred to as contract for sale of goods. The predominant feature of this type of contract is that it involves the selling of goods between the seller and commercial buyer. The purpose for which the goods are bought is of special relevance. This leads to the justification that the OHADA Uniform Sales law is entirely concerned with the reselling business of goods to non -consumers.[67] Again, undeniably, the idea connected with this issue of reselling of goods under the Uniform Act concerns expressly commercial buyers (acting as retailers or wholesalers), exercising trade for the purpose of the goods which are bought for resale and not for personal consumption.[68]

In a B2B contract under the Uniform Act, if a dispute arises that is not covered by the provisions of the Act, domestic law rules shall apply to

[63] See Article 44 UAGCL.
[64] See Article 46 UAGCL.
[65] Book II UAGCL; Article 6 Uniform Act on Commercial Companies and Economic Interest Groups.
[66] Articles 3–4 UAGCL.
[67] Article 235 para.1 UAGCL.
[68] Akuété Pedro Santos and Jean YadoToé, *OHADA Droit Commercial Général*, Collection Droit Uniforme Africain, Bruxelles, 2002, p. 341.

resolve the dispute.[69] These include the commercial code, the civil code or other national sources of law in force in the OHADA Contracting States. In practice, the civil code and the commercial code are the primary reference in term of B2B and B2C contracts.[70]

Business to Consumer

The Uniform Act expressly excludes business to consumer (B2C) contracts that is, a contract between a professional trader and a consumer.[71] As aforesaid, what the Uniform Act covers is a contract between two professionals, that is, a seller and a commercial buyer, acting in their usual business activities.[72]

As a matter of distinction, the Uniform Act expressly provides that a consumer is different from a trader (*commerçant*).It follows that a consumer is a person who buys goods for personal, family or household use[73] and not for purposes of buying and selling.[74] Therefore a consumer is neither a commercial operator nor a person acting within his professional capacity. In short, the consumer is outside the provisions on contract of sale governed by the Uniform Act and consequently, B2C contracts are undoubtedly not covered by the UAGCL.[75]

Even though in the past there has been an attempt to put in place a draft OHADA Uniform Act on Consumer Law[76], it could be inferred that the law governing B2C contracts in most OHADA Member countries are found in the ordinary law rules. The majority of these countries rely on Presidential decrees and ministerial orders rather than legislation to remedy the situation. Such countries include Cameroon,[77] Côte d'Ivoire[78] and Senegal.[79]

The reason for examining B2C contracts in the light of the OHADA Uniform Act on General Commercial Law, is because the usual transaction of the goods between the seller and the commercial buyer under the Act, is

---

69 Article 237 UAGCL.

70 For example, in Senegal, it is the Civil and Commercial Code of Obligations.

71 Article 235 (a) UAGCL.

72 Anne-Catherine Imhoff- Scheier, *Protection du Consommateur et Contrats Internationaux, (*Librairie de L'Université George & Cie S.A., Genève 2002) p. 76–95.

73 Article 235 (b) UAGCL.

74 Articles 1 and 3 UAGCL.

75 This is the same position under Article 2 of the CISG and the EC Directives on Unfair Contract Clause, See Official Journal, 1993 L-95/29–34, April 5, 1993.

76 Article 237 of the draft Uniform Act on Consumer Law.

77 see Cameroon, Law n°90/031, August 10, 1990 Organising Commercial Activities in Cameroon.

78 See Côte d'Ivoire, Article 1, loi n° 91–999 du 27 décembre 1991; *Pour la vente entre professionnel et consommateur*, (sales between professional traders),see Article 6–3 du décret 95–29 du 30 janvier 1995.

79 see Sénégal, loi n°94–63 du 22 aout 1994 sur le prix, la concurrence et le contentieux économique.

also by extension involves the reselling of those goods to the consumers who are the end-users of the goods. In fact, the very purpose for which the goods are bought under a sale contract is for resale with a view that of making profits. In other words, attention is given to consumers here because they buy directly from the ultimate commercial buyer, and consequently, what they can demand as quality matters to the commercial buyer. In another respect, the standard of determining resale here would be to distinguish between a retailer and a wholesaler. A retailer may normally sell to his usual customers, while a wholesaler usually has better access to different markets, for example, in different countries, and hence, to more or usual customers who may still be interested in the goods.[80]

The Legal Conception of Goods

'Goods' form the subject-matter of commercial sale contracts between the seller and the buyer which warrant the payment of a price. There is no definition of 'goods' in the UAGCL. Nor is it possible to deduce the meaning of the term by analysing different language versions of the statute. The Uniform Act seems to embody a rather conservative concept of 'goods', as it is considered both in legal writings and case law to apply basically to moveable tangible goods. Thus, according to most commentators intangible rights, such as patent rights, trademarks, copyrights, a quota of a limited liability company, as well as know-how, are not to be considered 'goods.' The same is true for immovable property.

Under the Uniform Act, the notion of 'goods' relates basically to movable and tangible objects. The notion of 'goods' serves to quantify the main obligation of the seller contained in Article 250, which requires that '... the seller must deliver the 'goods'... as required by the contract and this Uniform Act'. Therefore, to identify the ambit of the seller's conformance duty, it is relevant to identify the 'goods' that are the object of this Uniform Act. The term 'goods' is not defined in the Uniform Act as the case under the CISG.[81] However, its meaning can be understood by reference to the Uniform Act's Scope and General Provisions.[82] In particular, Article 234 (a) provides that "the provisions of this shall apply to contracts of sale goods", whereas Articles

80 Benjamin K. Leisinger, *Fundamental Breach: Considering Non-Conformity of the Goods*, (Sellier, European Law Publishers GmbH, Munchen 2007) p.47.

81 Article 30.

82 see Chapter 1.

235 and 236 restrict the ambit of the Act, and by implication, the ambit of 'goods'. By inference from the restrictions imposed by Article 236 UAGCL, it may be understood that the term 'goods' is fairly not extensive, indeed, virtually not all-embracing. It clearly excludes to a greater extent non-physical items, such as electricity, negotiable instruments, company shares, which are technically 'things in action' or incorporeal movables and so are excluded by the plain words of Article 236. Similarly, items of 'intellectual property' such as copyrights, patents and trade marks are not corporeal movables and so fall outside the definition, although of course goods may exist which embody these intellectual property rights as been discussed in chapter

The reason which may be advanced for dismissing intangible or immovable goods from the scope of the OHADA Uniform Act could be that even though these are assets available for trade, they can only be disposed by way of trade or security and not possibly to be transferred physically to another party. The absolute interest in such types of goods may be disposed of outright or may be made the subject of security. Since by virtue of Article 250 para. 1 UAGCL, the main duty of the seller under the contract of sale is to deliver the goods to the buyer, what matters here is the physical transferability of the goods and not necessarily the transfer of a legitimate interest in the goods. The peculiar consideration here does not lie on the identification of the type of goods but rather on the physical segregation and ownership of it. Only in this situation is segregation both possible and necessary to identify the subject of the transfer obligation of the seller under the Uniform Act.

In modern commerce, an important point , not yet resolved by the OHADA Uniform Act on General Commercial Law, is whether computer software may constitute 'goods' within the meaning of Article 234 para. 1. Software is normally embedded in some physical form, such as disks, or as part of a package in which it is sold along with computer hardware, that is, computers or computer parts. Therefore, it could be considered as a tangible object capable of it being possible to be transferable. This raises an argument in trying to understand why such an item cannot be considered as a 'good' under the Uniform Act. It could without any doubt be covered by the OHADA Uniform Act because such a good is being able to be transferred to another person in a contract of sale in its physical form. Again, there is probability that a disk be physically defective due to a virus for example. In this case, the seller should be liable as the seller of a physically defective car.

Under French law, goods are known as *marchandises*. This simply entails a collection of movable assets forming the subject-matter of a contract of sale. This is actually an element of *fond de commerce*. From this standpoint, there is one clear limit: this meaning will not include any form of immovable property in a contract of sale. Consequently, it can be inferred from the meaning of Article 235 para. 1 UAGCL that it limits the meaning of goods to movable property by its reference to *commerçants*. The meaning of 'sale of goods' limits the very meaning of 'goods'. Also, this would mean that no sale with a non-trader is of a 'good'. The general approach that is adopted under the Uniform Act is to apply the OHADA Uniform Act to the *commerçant* and not to *non-commerçant*.

The scope of the subject matter of contract of sale

Under the UAGCL and CISG, there is only one possible subject matter, which is goods, clearly because they are only concerned with the sale of goods contracts.

In this regard, the contract is valid under the three legal instruments even with a non-existent or impossible subject matter. It follows therefore that as a matter of similarity, the goods forming the subject-matter of the contract must be either existing or future goods in the formation of a contract of sale of goods. Existing or specific goods are goods identified and agreed upon at the time a contract of sale is made.[83]

To illustrate, the lack of the existence of goods in the formation of a contract of sale leads to remedies for non-performance, which is the same result under when the seller fails to transfer the property in the goods to the buyer because he or she lacks a legal title. To illustrate, if goods are perished at the time of contracting, then the contract is valid under the Principles. Nonetheless, the seller is unable to deliver them.

Existing goods

As a general rule of contract law, for an agreement for sale to be valid, the goods sold must exist. Existing goods may be either specific or unascertained. The main idea here is that the goods forming the subject-matter of the contract must be present and visible during the period of the formation of the contract. Existing or specific goods are goods identified and agreed upon at the time a contract of sale is made.[84] These are goods owned or in the seller's

[83] See SGA 1893 s 62 (1).

[84] See English Sale of Goods Act 1893 s 62 (1).

possession before or at the execution of the contract.[85] Similarly, as per the civil code, the goods, subject- matter of the transaction, must exist at the time of the execution of the contract.[86] Again, the presumption rests on the fact that for such a dealing to amount to a contract, the goods must be physically present under the seller's keeping and control.

Even though the Uniform Act does not clearly define what is a 'good(s)' under a contract of sale it covers, it would be understood to mean tangible goods necessary to conduct the business of sale of goods.[87]

The Uniform Act thus follows this position; it has already expressly identified the types of goods in a contract of sale it intends to cover [88] and by also excluding others which will not form a subject-matter of a sales contract.[89] This is another clear indication by inference of Article of 250 of the Uniform Act which considers the transfer obligation of the seller in a contract of sale of goods- meaning the existence of goods in their physical forms to the buyer together during the formation of the contract.[90]

Future goods

Generally, 'future goods' include goods not yet in existence and goods in existence but not yet in the seller's possession. It is prudent to say that future goods are not existing goods nor specific goods. Goods to be manufactured are a typical example of future goods or any goods that can only be acquired by the buyer after the contract of sale has been executed.[91] In accordance with the English Sale of Goods Act, these goods are existing or future goods and therefore can be the subject of a sales contract.[92] What may constitute future goods may be when a manufacturer agrees to build a specified piece of furniture, equipment or machine for sale to a customer.

Similarly, under the OHADA Uniform Act, these kinds of goods can form the subject-matter of sales contract especially when the goods must have been made available to the buyer to take delivery. One of the fundamental obligations of the seller is to hand over the goods to the buyer.[93] In reality, the

85 See English Sales of Goods Act 1893 s 5 (1).
86 Akuété Pedro Santos and Jean YadoToé, *OHADA Droit Commercial Général*, *op cit.*,p. 342.
87 *Ibid.*, p. 344.
88 Article 234 para.1 UAGCL.
89 Article 236 UAGCL.
90 Article 234.UAGCL.
91 SGA 1893 s 5 (1).
92 SGA 1893 s 5 (1).
93 Article 262 et seq. of the Uniform Act. (Article 267 is more illustrative).

buyer can only perform his payment obligation when the goods have been delivered to him in their physical state. Consequently, under the Uniform Act, it is possible for parties to enter into such an agreement for future goods. This position therefore follows the Common Law knowledge of specific and unascertained goods.

However, a distinction should be drawn between existing and future goods. Existing goods may be either specific or unascertained; while future goods are nearly always unascertained and specific goods are almost always existing goods. For example, a contract to sell a fungible item possessed in bulk by a seller in his store room will involve goods that are both existing and unascertained.[94]

Specific and unascertained goods

Specific goods or determined goods are goods identified and agreed on at the time a contract of sale is made, that is, a specific car.[95] Unascertained goods are those goods that, at the date of the contract, are not specific goods. Unascertained or generic goods, though not defined by the SGA have been referred to by scholars as goods to be manufactured which are necessarily future goods,[96] purely generic goods (10 kilos of rice) or an unidentified part of a specified whole (4 bottles of beer in a tray of 12 bottles of a different brand of beer).

The Uniform Act does not make references to ascertained goods, which are nowhere defined. By inference, however, like in most legal systems, it is a fundamental requirement in the sales contract that unascertained goods must be ascertained or ascertainable upon performance of the contract. As a matter of interpretation under Civil law, the "goods" must either be determined or subject to be determined.[97] Hence, it must be specific, stating for instance its specified name and if relevant with the quality, quantity or weight. But, if the contracting party fails to determine the quantity or quality of the goods, the civil code authorises a delivery of an average quality or quantity of the goods determined. The goods so identified are treated under the civil code as determined goods.[98]

---

94 Michael Bridge, The Sale of Goods, op.cit., p. 41

95 SGA 1979 s 61(1).

96 Roy Goode, *Commercial Law*, Oxford University Press, London, 2003, p. 210.

97 See Cameroon, Article 1129 CC; Côte d'Ivoire, Article 1129 CC; France, Article 1129 CC.

98 See Cameroon, Article 1126 CC; Côte d'Ivoire1126; France, Article 1126 CC.

Conclusion

The UAGCL has clearly identified the issue of consideration as primordial to the conclusion of a valid contract. Again, the rules relating to offer and acceptance are much more in line with the Civil law rather than Common law, and in many respects are much more closely attuned to commercial requirements.

3

QUALITY CONTROL OF GOODS

Introduction

The purpose of this chapter is to consider various problems concerning the quality of goods and show to an extent its interrelatedness with the pricing system in the market. There was an old doctrine of French law which holds that "sound price warrants sound article"[99]. But today, this doctrine is a sick horse. It is generally understood in the market that price which is apparently below than the actual value that it indicates, the buyer understands that he is receiving low grade of defective product. It is therefore necessary to have minimum standard of quality of goods which is to be sold in the market as merchantable.

The question of quality control is certainly one of the most important points arising in domestic and international contracts of sale of goods. In international sales the question becomes even more important as a result of geographical distance between the seller and the buyer and the fact that the goods are often transported through various climatic conditions may result in the quality of the goods delivered not conforming to that contracted for, particularly when those goods may be affected by the above mentioned factors. Hence it is not unusual for increased importance to be attached to the inspection of goods. Most often, consumer buyers of those goods are vulnerable to the poor quality of the goods. The rapid industrial development has not only brought new innovations and products into common use but has also affected the very quality of the goods. Consequently, in view of the socio economic changes which have taken place, it is imperative to build a strong based quality control mechanism which may give impetus and bring

[99] *Parkinson v. Lee* (1802) 2 East 314, 102 Eng. Rep. 389.

about socio legal measures necessary for trade and commerce as well as for consumer protection. This chapter aims to project the various problems surrounding the quality of goods, and to highlight to what extent, a balanced viewpoint can evolved in the business relationship between buyers and sellers within socio economic and legal framework of the society.

In order to gain a thorough insight into the question of inspection of goods, it is important to refer to various methods of quality determination agreed upon by the contracting parties the goods so that in inspection of the goods account is taken first of all of the intention of the contracting parties as expressed by them. Besides, if, however, the contracting parties have made no such determination of the quality of the goods, which are the subject matter of the contract of sale, the usual presumptions as regards quality would be whether the quality conforms to the standard of a national or international organisation or any third party employed by the contracting parties. However, it will be necessary in the first place to probe into the meaning of quality.

Determination of Quality

The numerous disputes involving the delivery of non-conforming goods as a result of low grade quality of goods boil down to the question of the seller's obligation of conformity of quality to be delivered as contained under the OHADA Uniform Act on General commercial Law. In order to deal with this point, however, it is necessary to consider how quality is determined, that is, what method, from the legal point of view, is applied in determining whether and to what extent the seller is liable for the quality of goods delivered which does not conform to the contract stipulations. The starting point in this analysis is the contract itself. However, a significant role in determining the quality of goods is played by mandatory (*ius cogens*) and standards (which, however, will not be discussed here).

Among these, two particularly important and complex sets of issues deserve further analysis both because they are resolved differently by different laws, and because they go to the heart of the conformity problem.[100] These are the questions of how to define the quality standard to which goods are to adhere, and what constitutes effective notice of non-conformity.

[100] Adam M. Giuliano, "Nonconformity in the Sale of Goods between the United States and China: The New Chinese Contract Law, the Uniform Commercial Code, and the Convention on Contracts for the International Sale of Goods," (2006) 18 *Florida Journal of International Law*, 331, p. 7.

Defining Quality

According to the Sale of Goods Act, the term "quality" refers to the state and condition of the goods.[101] At common law, there has sometimes been confusion between identification and quality. But in practice, it appears difficult to apply that distinction as similar facts resulting from the breach of quality[102] can also result in the breach of description or identity.[103] These provisions are exclusive at some points.[104] As a matter of fact, it may appear that a statement of quality regarding the goods form the descriptive part of the goods and vice versa.[105]

In *Toépfer v. Continental Grain Co*,[106] the word "hard" leading to the quality in the contract based on the "Hard Amber Durum Wheat" for the purpose of the finality of a certificate as to quality was, without doubt, also meant to describe the goods. Sometimes, the goods can be of such a poor quality that its description will rather amount to identify the goods than the quality of those goods. However, the quality of the goods per se can be determined differently. Under the SGA, there is no implied warranty or condition that goods supplied under the contract shall be of merchantable quality. So, the famous doctrine of *caveat emptor* (let the buyer beware) remains the guiding principle under certain circumstances where the provision of the Act applied.[107]As a principle of legal relationship between buyer and seller, *caveat emptor* is today a pretty sick horse. It is not so much the buyer as it is the manufacturer and the seller who must beware, on penalty of fine, or imprisonment.

Under the UAGCL, the notions of ''quality' and ''specification'' have also been a question as to the limit of one to the other.[108] The issue has generally been raised under Civil law. Hence, the notions of "quality" and "specification"[109] have been defined by French case law[110] and scholars[111] as different, but complementary. The reason is that the extent of the seller's

[101] SGA 1893 s 62.

[102] As per the breach of the implied condition as to the quality or fitness; SGA 1893 s 14.

[103] As per the breach of sale by description; SGA 1893 s 13.

[104] A.G.G Guest, *Benjamin's Sale of Goods, Op. cit.*, p. 545.

[105] As per the argument advanced in the leading case of *Ashington Piggeries Ltd v. Chrisptopher Hill Ltd*

[106] [1974] 1 Llyod'd Rep. 11.

[107] SGA 1893 s 14..

[108] Akuété Pedro Santos & Jean Yado Toe, *OHADA Droit Commercial Général, Op. cit*,. p. 394.

[109] Article 255 UAGCL.

[110] Civ.,4 déc. 1871., D.P., 1873, 5, 201.

[111] Gerard Cornu, *Vocabulaire Juridique*, (8 édition, Presses Universitaires de France, 1987) p. 756 ; Akuété Pedro Santos & Jean Yado Toé, *Op. cit.*, p. 394.

duty depends largely upon the meaning to be attached to the description of the goods. The view is that the OHADA Uniform Act does not provide any statutory meaning to the term 'quality' which has little substantive content. This tends to be meaningless in practice. It does not only suffice for the buyer to be entitled to goods which conform to quality. What is the buyer entitled to expect under the contract? As an answer to this, the buyer is entitled to expect goods of satisfactory quality, that is, goods suitable for reasonable usage. This reasonable use will certainly be for commercial re-saleability and not for personal consumption. This is the purport of Article 255 para. 2 of the UAGCL. The present provision provides that the quality of the goods includes their state and condition and that among other things which are aspects of the quality of goods for the purpose for which goods of the kind in question are commonly used. Clearly, fitness for all purposes is an important, indeed, an essential-element in the concept of conformity and remains important under the current provision of the Uniform Act.

The question arises whether the new provision of the Uniform Act clears up one major ambiguity which had previously been mentioned. Many goods are used for the variety of purposes, and the goods supplied under the contract may be fit for some of these purposes while unfit for others. The solution to this simply lies on the particular specification contained in a contract of sale provided by the buyer to the seller. This specification may among other things relate to the particular purpose the buyer wanted the goods for (in which case he could sue under Article 255 para. 1 UAGCL) as the goods are not of only merchantable but not satisfactory quality as well.

The UAGCL provides that, in the absence of agreement by the parties to the contrary, goods must be "fit for the purposes for which goods of the same description would ordinarily be used."[112] This standard "does not require that the goods be perfect or flawless, unless perfection is required for the goods to fulfill their ordinary purpose." On the other hand, what the standard positively requires regarding the minimum acceptable quality level remains unresolved. At least three standards have received support both from various courts and in academic literature; the standards are merchantable, average, and reasonable quality.[113] The first two standards depend upon standards and practices external to the parties, while the third standard relates in part to party expectations.[114]

112 Article 255 para. 2 UAGCL.

113 Adam M. Giuliano, "Nonconformity in the Sale of Goods between the United States and China: The New Chinese Contract Law, the Uniform Commercial Code, and the Convention on Contracts for the International Sale of Goods," *Op. cit.*, p.7

114 P.S. Atiyah, *The Sale of Goods*, *Op. cit.*, p.162.

Therefore, the phrase 'conformity' as used under the OHADA Uniform Act on General Commercial Law must be re-phrased to suit modern commerce and to avoid a litany of unnecessary cases to flood our law courts.[115] This is so because reference to conformity does not adequately convey the concept of acceptable quality of the goods. A particular attention should be given to the point under the UAGCL rather that making it cumbersome for one to clearly understand the seller's duty under the phrase "conformity". This is merely an umbrella term which embodies lots of issues to be deciphered by one's ingenuity. Regard should be paid to the change of this nomenclature introduced in England by the Sale and Supply of Goods Act 1994.[116] Goods are considered to be of satisfactory quality "if they meet the standard that a reasonable person would regard as satisfactory, taking account of any description of the goods, the price (if relevant) and all the other relevant circumstances". This suggests that description goes to the essence of what it is that the seller has contracted to sell, so that whether goods are of satisfactory quality almost inevitably depends on the description under which they are sold.[117]

In the opinion of P.S. Atiyah and others,[118] "all vague statements or definitions of the standard of quality required by the law, it may be suggested, are somewhat vacuous in practice". This suggests that these either concepts of satisfactory quality or conformity, should be replaced with concepts of reasonableness which have substantial flexibility. Most such standards give little guidance as to what kind of defects or damage will render goods not to conform (unsatisfactory under the SGA), and is unhelpful in the practical application of the law. All rely heavily upon the test of reasonableness: would a reasonable buyer, if he knew the condition of the goods, accept them under the contract? Would a reasonable buyer expect goods of that condition to be delivered under that sort of contract? Tests which depend so heavily upon standard of reasonableness tend to be somewhat circular in practice. In fact, the buyer is entitled to expect goods of quality and reasonable for that use. The "reasonable" use is the sort of the use which a reasonable buyer would intend.

If the quality of the goods has been accurately determined in the contract, the seller must comply with the detail criteria as strictly stated in the agreement and deliver the goods in conformity with the contract. Thus,

115 See the case of *Brasseries du Cameroun v. Ambe John*, Appeal No. BCA/8/93 24th March 1994, (unreported), in Juridis Périodique, (1997) No. 29–40 (A commentary by Ewang Sone Andy on the topic: "Brewed Drinks unfit for Human Consumption can Warrant an Action for Product Liability".

116 Atiyah et al., *The Sale of Goods, Op. cit.*, p.162; See Sections 14 (2) & 15 (2).

117 Roy Goode, *Commercial Law, Op. cit.*, pp.304–305.

118 *Ibid.*, p.174.

goods delivered with a quality higher or lower than the contract stipulation will not satisfy the requirement of conformity. By way of explanation, if the buyer requires Senegalese black wood to make a dugout, but received Kenyan black wood for a dugout, there will be defect on the quality of the goods. The notion of quality is therefore not restricted to the physical characteristics of the goods. It rather relates to some other aspects of quality which as a matter of importance concerns the fitness for the purpose(s) for which the commercial buyer under the UAGCL intends to use them.

To illustrate this point, in *Andrews Brothers (Bournemouth), Ltd. V. Singer & Co.*[119] a clause exempted all implied warranties and all liabilities. The court held that the clause did not apply to an express term describing the article in the contract and therefore, it did not exempt the seller from liability for delivering an article of a different description. Also, in *Henry Kendall & Sons v. William Lillico & Sons,*[120] there was a clause excluding liability for "latent defects" of goods. The House of Lords held that the expression "latent defects" only covered liability for the quality of the goods and did not exclude liability for breach of Section 14 (1) of the Sale of Goods Act 1893, that is, fitness for purpose.

Moreover, in addition to the quality of the goods, the usage intended for the goods shall also be satisfied otherwise, as conformity will not have been met. If the contract makes it clear that the Senegalese black wood is meant to build a dugout, if the wood, with the exact quality criteria as required has been provided, but turns out not to be able to make a dugout, there will be defect on conformity. Otherwise if the contract does not specify a precise usage, the ordinary usage of goods of the same kind must be satisfied.[121]

As a general rule under the UAGCL, conformity on the quality of the goods will be met if and only if their usage criterion is also satisfied.[122] It follows therefore that as a consequence of the non-conformity of the material or functional quality or of both, there is a breach of contract.[123] Moreover, if essential, such a breach may give rise to a fundamental breach,[124] enabling the buyer to avoid the contract[125] or to claim for substitute delivery.[126]

---

119 (1934) 1 K.B. 17.

120 1911 A.C. 394.

121 Akuété Pedro Santos & Jean Yado Toé, *OHADA Droit Commercial Général, Op. cit.*, p. 394–395.

122 Article 255 para. 2 UAGCL; As per the position in Cameroon, Article 1641 CC; Côte d'Ivoire, Article 1641 CC; France, Article 1641 CC.

123 Article 281 UAGCL; Article 45 CISG.

124 Article 281 UAGCL.

125 Article 283–284 UAGCL.

126 Article 283 UAGCL.

While uniformity does not exist regarding the applicable standard, the scope of this ambiguity is smaller than it appears. In most cases, the question of fitness for an ordinary purpose represents a factual question; in a given dispute, each of the possible quality standards might lead to the same conclusion. In the breach, the best guide to the appropriate quality level should be the parties' expectations.[127]For example, it has been argued that:

The role of Article 255 para. 2 UAGCL is to aid in construing the agreement of the parties. The question is this: What was the parties' understanding of the contract provision describing the goods? More precisely (in the language of Article 255 para.2 UAGCL), what was their understanding of the 'purposes for which goods of the same description would ordinarily be used'? Since the problem concerns fitness for the 'ordinary' use of goods described in the contract, serious misunderstandings should be infrequent.

The view that the parties' agreement cabins the quality standard under Article 255 para. 2 UAGCL gains support both from the Article's text, which references the goods' "description." This is in line with the Secretariat Commentary to the draft CISG. The Secretariat Commentary balances such party expectations with a kind of reasonableness level commensurate with the ordinary use of the good, stating that "the standard of quality which is implied from the contract must be ascertained in the light of the normal expectations of persons buying goods of this contract description."

Aspects of Quality

It is worth at this point to examine some characteristics of quality in relation to the goods sold by the seller with a view to ascertain the extent of the seller's liability. Should the seller be expected to always sell goods of first or best quality? What does the buyer expect of the quality of the goods?

Liability for Commercial Seller's for Used –Goods

One still remains baffled about whether strict liability should apply to commercial sellers of used products. The expectation of the quality of these types of goods is usually not the same as those newly sold. From the text of the Uniform Act, liability will be imposed on "regular" used-goods sellers. Several field trips by this researcher reveal that used-product markets

[127] Adam M. Giuliano, *Op. cit.*, p.7.

are common in the major cities of Cameroon in particular and in some African Countries.[128] These goods vary from cars, household equipments to consumer goods. It is an everyday practice now to find a line-up of stores in the towns of Douala and Yaoundé operating in this trade. Observation from this experience reveals that consumers prefer and expect diminished quality and safety from used goods. This is because of the cheap prices of these goods and their accessibility. Another justification for this is the public habits and beliefs in certain virtues of these goods which have stood their test of time. Such a picture is typical in Cameroon where from socio-economic and psychological perspectives, the purchasing public still hold tight to the buying of some goods of old reputable trade mark or taste. For example, certain brand of goods such as, shoes like "pierre cadin" from France, "clarks" from England are still believed to be durable even sold as a used goods.

It is staggering to note that the magnitude of this problem of used-goods may be better appreciated by bearing in mind the potential problem of product dumping from countries with stricter safety laws.[129] It is not inconceivable for unscrupulous foreign manufacturers to target the markets of developing countries with products that fail to meet the safety requirements in terms of their period of expiration or damaged in their packing of their home countries by charging low prices for these products in the importing country. Banned or used-goods are dumped in developing countries through a number of ways. This is effected either simply through changing the product's name or slightly altering the chemical formula or subtracting an inert part of the good. Sometimes the parts of the banned product are then exported separately to the country, where a recombining facility is set up for assembly. It could be said that most of the components of these products are used to build up a "new" structure. These unscrupulous businessmen would close down their plants at home and establish more lucrative business in third world countries, where they can freely manipulate with products of low quality and sell those whose shelf-lives have expired in their home countries.

Used-product sellers serve an essential role in fostering an efficient economy. They help businesses and government's recycle, which reduces the cost and environmental impact of the manufacture of new products. By broadening the reasonable standard of care of used-product sellers, courts should recognise these legitimate social benefits of a used-product

[128] Specifically in some major markets in Abidjan-Côte d'Ivoire and Accra-Ghana, where research was conducted by the author.

[129] Samgena D. Galega, "Strict Liability for Defective Products in Cameron? Some Illuminating Lessons from Abroad", *Op. cit.*, p. 253.

market.[130] However, expanded absolute liability should force used-product sellers to act as virtual insurers for any kind of latent defect.[131] This justification should also rest on the fact that it should be maintained because of breach of the duty of conformity as well as misrepresentation in accordance with rules under the Uniform Act. Regard should not be given to the new or old state of the goods but much attention should be paid to the economic value incurred by the commercial buyer and the personal injury to the consumer. By imposing this liability on the used-product sellers, it will force manufacturers or suppliers of goods to discard these types of businessmen from their business line because they are unable to guarantee the safety and quality of those goods, which may tend to drive similar products of the same brand from the market. Thus, such a measure would make manufacturers to stand behind the goods they sell in the marketplace. As a mate of public policy, to properly price all goods according to their true social and economic costs, liability must apply to all sellers of defective goods. Otherwise, one defective product seller would cost relatively less, thereby encouraging consumers to buy the cheaper, more dangerous products. A used- product seller is no different from a new-product seller, and therefore, is liable for the sale of defective goods. Only the imposition of liability on sellers' of used-goods can effectively deter the spread of defective goods.

Consequently, making a market incentive to sell quality used-products would increase the likelihood that consumers will buy quality used-products from retail or wholesale buyers who may stand as proxy for product quality.[132] A seller interested in providing its customers with a product whose performance will fully meet both the needs of the latter might be able to establish a system of quality control that would eliminate the risk that deficient products would be delivered to customers. An alternative approach would be to use less stringent quality control practices and compensate buyers for defects in products when buyers discern those defects and complain about them.[133]

Consider the current market in which goods are sold honestly or dishonestly; quality may be represented, or it may be misrepresented. The

130 J. Paul Peter & Jerry C. Olson, *Consumer Behavior and Marketing Strategy*, (2nd edition, Homewood 1998) pp. 496–510.

131 Antonio J. Senagore, "The Benefits of Limiting Strict Liability for Used-Product Sellers", (2010) *30 Northern Illinois University Law Review*, pp.1–34, p. 3.

132 *Ibid.*, p. 12.

133 Arthur Best & Alan R. Andreasen, "Consumer Response to Unsatisfactory Purchase: A Survey of Perceiving Defects, Voicing Complaints, and Obtaining Redress", (1977) 11 *Law & Society*, pp. 701–742, p. 703.

commercial buyer's problem, of course, is to identify quality. The presence of sellers in the local markets who are willing to offer inferior goods tends to drive the market of some specific brand of goods out of existence – as is the case of bad automobiles or building construction materials. In *Scholastic Nsaiboti v. Felix Ezeafor*[134], the appellant bought a second –hand car from the respondent car dealer who made oral representations to the effect that the car was one year old and in good working condition. The oral representation proved to be untrue since the car was indeed older than that and was utterly defective. The contract, however, contained a term that excluded liability for any defect in the car and for any implied express warranty. The Bamenda Court of Appeal (in the English speaking region of Cameroon), in upholding the High Court's decision in favour of the respondent had this to say: "Restricted though the doctrine of 'caveat emptor' might be in its application to contracts of sale, its application in the buying of a second-hand car is in my opinion most fitting since there is very little by way of guarantee that the seller could give as to fitness" – per Rupert Thomas J., President of the Court.

If the above case shows the courts in dealing with the problem of the sale of second-hand cars, the case of *Michael Ebwe v. Hubert Euverte*[135] accentuates this point. On the 13th of May 1974, at about 10 a.m., the plaintiff entered into a written contract with the defendant for the sale of a second-hand car. The contractual document stipulated that the buyer has been given the opportunity of examining the car and that any liability whatsoever was excluded. The plaintiff signed the contractual document allegedly without reading it. On the same day the sale took place, at about 5 p.m., the car's engine stalled and the car was, on later examination, proved to be considerably defective. The plaintiff tried to get a refund of the contract price from the defendant on the grounds that the car was worthless, whereupon he brought this action. The Buea High Court held that the terms of the contract were clear and wholly unambiguous and that in the absence of fraud, they were binding on the parties.

It is this possibility that represents the major costs of dishonesty - for dishonest dealings tend to drive honest business dealings of some goods out of the market. There may be potential buyers of good quality products and there may be potential sellers of such products in the appropriate price range; however, the presence of dishonest sellers who wish to pawn bad wares as good wares tends to drive out the legitimate business, causing scarcity. The cost of dishonesty, therefore, lies not only in the amount by which the buyer

134 Appeal No. BCA/6/73 of March 1974, Bamenda Court of Appeal (unreported).
135 Suit No. HCSW/24, 1974, Buea High Court (unreported).

is cheated; the cost also must include the loss incurred from reducing the size of the legitimate business of certain goods out of the market.

It is now a common practice in most countries that before goods are sold nationally or internationally, they should meet the minimum ethical and quality requirements. This could be inspected by the contracting parties as they deem it necessary for this to be conducted by a third party.

Ethical values

It is wrong to think that business is incompatible with ethics. Ethical value is an emerging applied subject. It is still currently debated as it is applied to all aspects of business conduct and getting much more relevant to the conduct of individuals, the manufacturing of goods and the quality standard of goods. In general, ethical values appear to contribute to the development of legal systems in which contracts are enforced fairly, and bribery and corruption are less prevalent, enabling business entities to have equal access to legal process and equal protection under the law.

At the international level for instance, private initiatives such as the principles laid down in the United Nations Global Compact covering issues such as human rights, labour, environment and anti-corruption aim to assist its member countries to comply with the international standards required on these issues.

Although these are not yet much debated to prevent corruption, promote fair dealing and ensure a standard ethical quality. In Africa, ethical values are known and recognised in international and national sales contracts as one of the solutions to the defective goods as from the manufacturing process.

An ethical value contractual clause can be express or implied in the contract of sale. When implied, they may be inferred from trade and usages. Whether expressly or impliedly in a contract of sale, they become part of the contract and may be enforced, or their violation sanctioned, in the same way as with any other term. However, the parties agree on their express stipulation.[136]

In Cameroon, for instance, most organised professions and some trade associations have codes of practice which set out ethical behaviour for members in their dealings with their clientele.[137] For instance, the company

136 Peter H. Schlectreim, "Non-Material Damages - Recovery under the CISG?", (2007) Reproduced with permission of 19 *Pace International Law Review*, p. 89–102, point III (3). see <http://www.cisg.law.pace.edu/cisg/biblio/schlechtriem15.html>.

137 These would include the code of ethics of manufacturers' associations, association of advertising practitioners, etc.

in charge of distributing energy[138] makes available to the public an e-mail address for anyone who wants to make a complaint and report any violations of their Code of Business Conduct and Ethics. A clause ensuring ethical code and conduct is prior inserted in the contract signed by customers, before they benefit from the services of the company. This is done in favour of its customers.

In line with the above example, it should be pointed out that in most, if not all contracts of sale of goods, including both domestic or international contracts, the quality of goods is not restricted to its physical appearance; it also has to comply with any other requirements which are prescribed by the law or subject to trade usages.[139] Therefore, if the origin of the goods prescribes an ethical value standard at production, the standard will definitely constitute a quality of the goods. As a result, the requirement of quality will not be met if the goods produced do not meet with the ethical standard as required.

It is not easy to determine the non-conformity of goods based on the ethical value.[140] Such difficulty is due to the hidden character of its nature and also to the fact that it does not physically influence the physical feature of the goods. If the party in breach does not in good faith disclose or cure the defect, an expert may sometimes be required to determine the breach.

Unless the parties have agreed otherwise, failure from the seller to deliver the goods in conformity with the ethical standards amounts to a breach of contract. In particular, this is so when the seller is required to deliver goods that are fit for the purpose for which goods of that nature are commonly used or when a special request on an ethic (such as health and environmental considerations) was made known to the seller.[141] The buyer's remedy will be rights of redress[142] and claim for damages.[143]

Good Manufacturing Practice (GMP)

"Good Manufacturing Practice" (GMP) is a well-known policy whose purpose is to ensure appropriate manufacturing process that would impact on the quality of the products. Good Manufacturing Practice is a series of policies that are binding on the contracting business parties, (if agreed)

138 This para-statal company is known as AES- SONEL.
139 Article 238 -239 UAGCL.
140 Article 255 para. 1 UAGCL.
141 Article 255 para. 2 UAGCL.
142 Article 282–283 UAGCL.
143 Article 292–293 UAGCL.

requiring food producers, manufacturers, pharmaceutical companies[144] and packagers of drugs to ensure that their products are safe, pure and totally effective. These measures are meant to ensure a level of quality approach to manufacturers of goods in order to protect consumers from contracting for non-effective and dangerous goods. In summary, Good Manufacturing Practice plays a paramount role of quality assurance that ensure that products are consistently produced and controlled with respect to the quality standards appropriate for their intended use and their legal requirements or simply as required by the marketing board or in some countries by the government department in charge of regulating trade and commerce.

Sometimes, GMP is referred to as cGMP meaning "Current Good Manufacturing Practice". This is a mere call to producers, packagers or manufacturers to update their machineries, systems or equipment in order to comply with the new technology, capacity and /or legal requirement in their business. Generally, GMP's guidelines provide regulation on products such as foods, drugs, blood, and medical devices. Accordingly, countries do update their cGMP regulations for local companies to act in accordance with the legislation. In medicine, for instance, the Medicines Control Council (MCC) is a statutory body that was established in terms of the medicines and related substances control to oversee the regulation of medicines in South Africa.[145] The role of the MCC is to ensure that all medicines that are sold and used in South Africa are safe, therapeutically effective and consistently meet acceptable standards of quality. A series of other cGMP are enforced in South Africa[146] and across the region[147] to ensure the effectiveness of the quality of the goods. Particularly in Cameroon, the "Standard and Quality Agency (ANOR)" and the "Service de la Normalisation" in the Ministry of Trade and Commerce have the mandate to ensure the quality of products in meeting

---

144 Definition of GMP by the World Health Organisation and as per GMP institute found at <http//www.gmp1st.com/index.htm> (Last accessed on 24/10/09).

145 South Africa, Known as MCC; Act, 101 of 1965.

146 (South Africa); Regulations relating to the fortification of Foodstuffs, under the Foodstuffs, Cosmetics and Disinfectants Act 1972, Act N°54; Regulations Governing Microbiological Standards for Foodstuff and related Matters, promulgated under the notice N° R. 692 of 16 May 1997 and amended recently under the notice N° Notice No. R.490 of 8 June 2001; Regulations Relating to Milk and Dairy Products, promulgated under the notice N°R. 1555 of 21 November 1997 and amended under the notice N° R.489 of 8 June 2001; Regulations under the Food, Drugs and Disinfectants Act (Act No.13 of 1929).

147 Kenya, Pharmacy and Poisons Act 1972; Kenya, Tanzania; Uganda, Fish and Fishery Products (AFIPEK 2000) for handling and processing fish and fishery products in Kenya; (Sénégal), Arrêté Ministériel no. 2004–099 du 14 janvier portant application des bonnes pratiques de fabrication des médicaments, Loi N°54 -418 du 15 Avril 1954 portant code de la santé Publique dans les Territoires d'Outre Mer.

required standards.[148]At the continental level, the "African Organisation for Standardisation" also acts as a watchdog in ensuring quality goods and services in its member States. In Nigeria, the National Agency for Food and Drug Administration and Control (NAFDAC),[149] has the burden to regulate, control and process the quality standards for Foods, Drugs, Cosmetics, Medical Devices, Chemicals, Detergents and packaged water imported, manufactured locally and distributed in Nigeria.

Even though not prescribed by the UAGCL, such a business practice or measure is relevant in enhancing the warranty of quality of goods which flood the markets. This goes a long way to improve on the quality of goods which the end- users would obtain from commercial buyers. A respect of such a measure is left to the wishes of the parties in a contract of sale or could be implied from the trade usage of specific goods in a given branch of business. This is the very meaning of Articles 237 and 239 of the UAGCL.

Quality of Goods Expressly Determined by the Contract

Contracting parties may, in a contract of goods may, as already mentioned determine the quality of goods in various ways. This will often depend on the kind of goods and the purpose for which they are being purchased. The basic rule is that if a precise specification of the goods is given, (this concerns generics goods), the quality must conform to that described in the contract. The explicit determination of quality in the contract will be done by referring to the sample.

Sale by Sample as elusive method of determining the quality and properies of the goods

Sale by sample is most often employed in respect of the sale of generic goods. Instead of describing the subject-matter of the contract, the contracting parties may determine that quality should be identical to that of sample. This type of sale is particularly common in cases of sale through agencies, travelling salesmen who bring small quantities of articles that can give the

[148] This Ministry was created by Decree No.88/204 of 5 February 1988, re-organising the Ministry of Commerce. This full text of this Ministerial Decree is found in *Juridis Périodique* , no. 5, 1991, p.13. These structures were created with the objective of protecting consumers and ensuring the technical supervision of the quality and quantity of goods through inspection.

[149] Decree N° 15 of 1993 as amended by Decree N° 20 of 1999.

prospective buyer a complete picture of the quality and other properties of the goods.[150]

Under the UAGCL, like it is the case under Common law, it must be mphasized that where a description of the quality of the goods is given, the sample will be considered to have been used for identification of the goods or determination of their quality and properties. In other words, if the goods delivered do not conform to the sample, the Uniform Act will regard this act on the part of the seller as lack of conformity. What is essential is whether the sample has been used as a term of the contract or not. The goods do not conform with the contract unless they possess the qualities of goods which the seller has held out to the buyer as a sample or model.[151] Thus, from the provisions of the UAGCL, it can be understood that in a contract of sale, the sample is the exclusive standard of quality of the goods and, in such a case, any variation from the sample entitles the buyer to repudiate the contract. There is insistence on the full conformity of the goods to the sample (if so contracted).

Unfortunately, the Uniform Act is silent on cases where the sample or model is shown during negotiations but there is no reliable proof in the contract thereof nor can it be proved with certainty in some other way that the parties intended the quality of the goods to conform to the sample in every respect. The UAGCL does not contain any provision on sale by sample used unconditionally in respect of full conformity. However, much regard should be given to the intent and conduct of the parties during the bargaining phase. Nevertheless, from the spirit of the law, the sample is an appropriate method of determining quality and property in the goods by the buyer under the Act in consideration of the very purpose of goods which the commercial buyer desires to use in his business. Therefore, the seller shall be held liable for non-conformity if the goods delivered do not correspond to the sample.

Another important consideration that arises is whether sale by sample entitles the buyer to make a case against the seller for inherent vice if the goods delivered correspond to the sample. Under the UAGCL, this kind of a problem does not prevent the buyer from having recourse to the remedies available for cases of inherent vice.[152] Furthermore, the Uniform Act imposes on the seller the duty to provide guarantee for the goods.[153] Presumably, this is whether the sale is by sample or not. This protects the buyer because goods

150 Stoljar Samuel J., "Conditions, Warranties and Description of Quality in Sale of Goods", *Op. cit.*, p.443–446.

151 Article 255 UAGCL.

152 Articles 256–259 UAGCL.

153 Article 260 para. 1 UAGCL.

sold by sample must necessarily be suitable for resale. Accordingly, regardless of the fact that the sample had a latent defect, there is a presumption that the goods must be of merchantable quality.

In Common law jurisdictions, sale by sample is governed by the SGA.[154] There is a contract for sale by sample when there is an express or implied term to that effect in the contract. In respect of sale by sample, English law provides "an implied condition that the goods be free from any defect rendering them unmerchantable which would not be apparent on reasonable examination of the sample".[155] Thus, if any sample is made as part of the contract of sale, it creates an essential condition of the contract, that is, an express warranty that the goods shall correspond to the sample.[156] In short, whether there exists a contract of sale by sample is a question of law and not a question of fact. In other words, the fact that a seller provides to the buyer an item for inspection does not, *ipso factor*, amount to sale by sample, unless there is evidence of a clear intention of the parties to contract as such.[157] Similarly, in case of a contract in writing, there must be written evidence that the parties intended to be contracted as such. It follows that parol evidence when contract is in writing will be inadmissible in determining whether or not there was a sale by sample.[158] Therefore, for an effective sale by sample, the parties must either expressly or by implication make it clear as was stated in the case of *Ernest Friedrischdorf and Co v. Fuja*.[159]

However, the exception in the latter point may occur in circumstances where the contract of sale is backed up by custom or usage of trade. Here, it is immaterial whether the contract itself makes reference of the sample.[160] Once it has been legally established that there is a sale by sample, the statute (SGA) provides a series of implied terms that must be considered. First, there is an implied condition that the goods shall correspond with the sample in quality.[161] In other words, the bulk and the sample shall match each other. In *Warwick v. Mackenzie Co Ltd*,[162] the court pointed out that for a sale by sample to be made, the parties must have contracted with reference to a sample and with a common understanding that the sample constitutes the description of the goods to be purchased.

[154] SGA 1893 s 15.
[155] See Section 15(2) (6) SGA
[156] See also similarly the American Uniform Commercial Code (Section 2–313).
[157] P.S. Atiyah et al., *The Sale of Goods, Op. cit.*, p. 212–213.
[158] *Ginner v. King* (1890) 7 TLR 140.
[159] [1967] LLR 115.
[160] *Seyers v. Jones* [1848] 154 ER 426.
[161] SGA 1893 s 15 (2) (a).
[162] [1921] 2 W.N.R.

Sometimes the contract determines the limit of the description in a sale by sample. For instance, if the contract states that the bulk shall correspond in type and quality to the sample, whatever fault and value the bulk might have will in no way effect a breach of the contract of sale.[163] It might appear that the sample does not dictate for it itself but rather that, the contract defines the criteria of the bulk. Second, it is an implied term that the buyer shall have a reasonable opportunity of comparing the sample with the bulk.[164] Reasonable inspection by the buyer of both the bulk and the sample should reveal any defect. If this opportunity is offered, the buyer is usually bound as was the case in *Lorymer v. Smith*[165]. Third, there is an implied term that goods shall be free from any defect rendering them unmerchantable, which would not be apparent on reasonable examination of the sample.[166] The case implied term was laid down in the case of *Godley v. Perry*,[167] where the breach of conformity of the sale by sample was clearly established.[168] In this case, a child, after a careful look at the sample, went ahead and purchased the plastic toy catapult which he examined by pulling back its elastic. The elastic cut and injured him on the eye. Such a defect would not therefore have been apparent by a mere examination of the good.

Determination of the Quality if not provided for in the Contract (Tacit Conditions of Quality of Goods)

As it is often done in business operations, the contracting parties may make no precise statement regarding the quality of the goods and then the question arises as to of what quality the goods must be if they are not rejected by the buyer.

One way the seller may satisfy the functional conformity,[169] is for him to be able to guarantee that there are no hidden defects on the goods.[170] However, it should be pointed out that a hidden defect, as provided in the Uniform Act, does not only relate to the non-conformity but also to the usage as well.[171] By

[163] *Champanthac & Co Ltd v. Waller & Co Ltd* (1979) 1K.B 254 at.260.
[164] SGA 1893 s 15 (2) (b).
[165] (1822) 1 B & C 1.
[166] SGA 1893 ss 15 (2) (c).
[167] [1887] 12 App. Cas. 284, at. 297.
[168] SGA 1893 s 15 (2) (c).
[169] Article 255 para. (1) and (2) UAGCL.
[170] Mevoungou Nsana Roger, "Les Obligations du Vendeur de Marchandises dans l'Acte Uniforme OHADA", *Op. cit.*., pp.8–12.
[171] Meaning that there is no conformity when the defect affects the usage of the goods.

way of explanation, the goods should conform to the general usage of such goods or the particular usage for which the buyer expressly intended the goods for. It is implicit from this standpoint that the implied duties of the seller, codified in Article 255 UAGCL, is no less than the seller's implied promise that the goods sold in a contract of sale will work. It is a warranty that arises as an operation of law, as opposed to an affirmative promise from the seller, and simply codifies the parties' expectations of what the goods are for and what they will accomplish for the buyer.[172] In this way, the implied condition of "conformity" in the Uniform Act gives teeth to the bargain and provides the buyer with one method for forcing the seller to behave properly. As the seller is a merchant, the buyer's expectation is to benefit from the promise that the goods will fulfill the basic function of their ordinary purpose.

Fitness for Particular Purpose

The UAGCL clearly states that goods under the contract of sale are fit for the specific or particular purpose provided the seller knew of this at the time of the conclusion of the contract.[173] The aim is to protect any buyer who acquires goods by informing the seller on the particular purpose and purposes on which the goods will be used for. In reality, it appears that the requirement for goods fit for ordinary use overlaps with that on the fitness for a particular purpose. Nevertheless, two elements constitute their distinction: first, the requirement for the fitness for particular purpose must only be used where the buyer makes known to the seller the specific or particular purpose for which he intends to use the goods. It follows therefore that accuracy the particular information of the goods, will aid the seller to satisfy the buyer's need.

The second aspect concerns reliance. As a professional businessman, the seller is an expert in the field of the goods contracted by the buyer, and latter usually relies on the seller's skill to provide him with the exact goods requested.

In accordance with the SGA, whenever the buyer, expressly or by impliedly, makes known to the seller the particular purpose for which the goods are required, there is an implied condition that the goods shall be reasonably fit for such purpose. As a matter of fact, the buyer relies on the seller's skill or judgment, and the goods are of a description which it is in the course of the

[172] Franklin E. Crawford, "Fit for its Ordinary Purpose? Tobacco, Fast Food, and the Implied Warranty of Merchantability", (2002) 63 *Ohio State Law Journal*, 1165, p.2.

[173] Article 255 para.2 UAGCL.

seller's business to supply (regardless of whether he is the manufacturer or not). However, there is no implied condition as to its fitness for any particular purpose over the sale of a specific article under its patent or other trade name.[174]

A distinction has to be made between fitness for a particular purpose as opposed to general purpose. Firstly, within the meaning of the provision, "particular purpose" shall be understood to be "specific purpose";[175] notwithstanding that the purpose may be a general one, for instance, a cloth to wear. In *Mac Gill v. Tailbot*[176] a car collector made known to the car seller that he wanted a Rolls Royce car that was reasonably fit for the purpose of economic restoration. It was held that the purpose for which the car was to be used in this case was communicated.

But, in *Manchester Liners v. Rea Ltd*[177], it was held that no express disclosure is necessary if the seller is aware of the particular purpose for which the goods are required. He might be aware due to his knowledge of past transactions or by the implied nature of the goods. It follows that the disclosure of the particular purpose of the goods can be made either expressly or in circumstance that let the buyer beware that he relies on the seller's skill and judgement.[178]

In *Ijomo v. Mid Motors Nigeria Ltd*,[179] there was no breach of contract as to the implied condition on quality or fitness of the goods.[180] Thus, Lagos High Court established that there was no evidence at all as to whether the buyer informed the seller of the purpose for which the cars were bought. The reliance on the seller can therefore either be express[181] or implied and such reliance must have induced the buyer to enter into contract. The reliance is not subjective but rather objective as it is generally a matter of inference because what matters is what a reasonable man in the position of a seller would have realised, by relying or not on the purpose of the goods made known to him. Lastly, with regard to the fitness for particular purpose, it is being considered by case law that it is a relative issue that does not depend either on the objective or the subjective contemplation between the parties

174 SGA 1893 s 14 (1).
175 *Kendall v. Lillico* (1969) 2 AC 31, 123 as per Lord Wilberforce.
176 2002 GWD 12–382 (Sherriff G. J. Evans).
177 [1922] 2 A.C.74 .
178 Igweike K.I., *Sales of Goods, Nigerian Commercial Law, Op. cit.*, p. 54–55.
179 CCHCJ / 9/ 754 p. 1326.
180 SGA 1893 s 14 (1).
181 For instance the particular purpose is mentioned in the contract as in the case of *Manchester Liners v. Rea Ltd., Op. cit.*

but rather on factual and material circumstances of each case.

In *Onutu v. Adeleke and Another*,[182] the Kaduna High court held that because the car was broken five days after the day it was purchased while driven on the road, the requirement of fitness of the particular purpose of the car as stated in the contract of sale was not satisfied. The buyer in contracting with the seller asked for a new car but the seller sold him a second-hand car. It is not reasonable for a new car to be broken after five days of being driven. It is important to note that there is no implied condition that the goods shall fit absolutely to the particular purpose expressly nor impliedly determined. If, for instance, an unusual consequence occurs producing an unexpected accidental injury, as a result of an undisclosed information regarding a defect in the good by the buyer which was not known to the seller, the latter will not be held liable in the circumstances as it was decided in the case of *Griffiths v. Peter Conway Ltd.*[183]

Fitness for ordinary use

Lord Diplock's statements in the case of *Ashington Piggeries v. Christopher Hill Ltd*,[184] defines fitness of goods for ordinary use as goods of a kind, those verbally identified by a description that is wide enough to include goods which are intended for use for the particular purpose for which the buyer requires the goods, which are the subject matter of the contract.

In various countries having adopted the SGA,[185] particularly on the question of the fitness for ordinary use, the Act states that, where the buyer, expressly or by implication, makes known to the seller the purpose for which the goods are required, so as to show that the buyer relies on the seller's skill or judgment, and the goods are of a description which it is in the course of the seller's business to supply, there is an implied condition that the goods shall reasonably be fit for that purpose. Thereon, it is immaterial whether or not the seller is a manufacturer of the goods.[186] This position has been complemented by case law interpretations in practice.

Under the UAGCL, the delivery of goods in a sale contract does not satisfy the requirement of conformity unless and until they are fit for the purpose

182 [1975] N.L.R. 130.

183 [1939] 1 All ER 685; same decision in *Ingham v. Ernes* (1955) 2 Q.B. 366.

184 *Op. cit.*

185 Cameroon, Botswana, Ghana, Kenya, Malawi, Mozambique, Namibia, Nigeria, Tanzania, Uganda, Zimbabwe, Zambia,

186 George Gleason Bogert, "Express Warranties in Sales of Goods", *Op. cit.*, p.17; 14 (1) SGA 1893 s 14 (1).

and purposes for which goods of the same description would normally be used.[187] Therefore, this raises the problem of measuring how the fitness of the ordinary use is met. Accordingly, it is advanced that an objective test should be used to determine the ordinary use. Thus, whether or not the goods are fit for the purpose and purposes for which goods of such description are ordinarily used, must be determined in light with what a reasonable person in the same trade as the parties to the contract would best do.[188]

However, if any precise purpose was brought to the knowledge of the seller[189] at the time of the conclusion of the contract, goods which do not serve the precise purpose will be considered as being not in conformity with contract even if the ordinary purposes do exist.[190] Generally, for the purpose of convenience, courts are required to first attempt to determine whether any indication as to the usage[191] of the goods was brought to the seller's attention before seeking a reasonable man position as to what amounts to the ordinary use[192].

Usual Packaging and its Importane for the Quality of Goods.

In the modern turnover of goods, the importance of packing is considerable. Its purpose is not to protect the product but also to present it to the buyer in unattractive manner. Thus packing, particularly that of consumer goods becomes a factor in the good marketing of goods. However, it is important to point out that packing requirements are loosely connected with the delivery of the goods so that any packing defects may become quality defects of the goods, particularly when the goods are sold in the so called "original packing" (tins, cans, tubes etc) without which they would not be put on sale. In the latter case, the packing is "incorporated" into the goods and is considered to be an integral part of the very goods to be delivered. With the specific type of goods intended for human consumption the regulations on quality include the packing as well. For example, the regulations governing meat, fish and cereals determine precisely in what packing they may be delivered. Of recent, the government has embarked on strict use of bio graderable waterproof paper for such goods. Though such a measure has been made by

187 Article 255 para. 2 UAGCL.
188 Articles 238 para. 1 & 239 UAGCL.
189 Article 255 para. 2 UAGCL.
190 Article 255 para.2 UAGCL.
191 Article 238 para. 2 UAGCL.
192 Article 238 para.1 UAGCL.

the government, traders continue to undermine it.

The same is true of goods in general; the use and quality of the packing may also be regulated and the seller is bound to observe those regulations, as the products in question cannot otherwise be put on sale. In this regard, standards and usages may also exist and the seller (or the buyer, depending on who is to provide the packing according to the contract) is bound to observe those standards or usages. Similarly, under the UAGL, unless and until the goods are packaged in accordance with the contract, there is non-conformity of the goods.[193] This seller's obligation is therefore emphasised in the same provision which requires that, in the absence of a contrary stipulation between the parties, the goods must be packaged or contained in the usual method of packaging goods of the same nature, or in a manner to ensure their conservation and protection.[194]

It should be emphasised that courts and arbitrators often face the difficulty of determining what constitutes "usual" packing. The question is particularly complex in connection with international transport where, owing to long journeys, goods may be damaged, especially if not packed properly. This also concerns long distance transportation of goods within the country. In the sale of fruit and fresh fish for example, regarded as easily perishable goods, special attention is paid to the packing. It is usually stressed that the packing and manner of pacing must conform to the weather conditions at the time of delivery. Whether the fruit of fish will have to be transported in special refrigerated trucks will depend on each case and the type of perishable goods involved.

The test for usual packaging is that of a reasonable man, in the same trade or transactions, in addition to any relevant trade usages.[195] But generally, as to the question regarding what package is adequate for the goods, the answer will depend on the nature, descriptions and/or conditions of the goods in every contract of sale.

Generally, after seeing the sample of the bulk, the buyer is expecting to receive goods identical to the sample he had inspected. In other words, the goods have to correspond with the description or the sample. Thereof, the packaging must also be accurate. The SGA at this instance makes it clear that where there is a contract for sale by description, there is an implied condition

193 Article 255 para. 2 UAGCL.

194 *Ibid.*, UAGCL ; See also the publication of Centre *du Commerce International sur La Promotion de L'Emballage pour L'Exportation*, Volume I : Guide des mesures institutionnelles a aprendre et de l'assistance technique, Genève, 1975.

195 Articles 238 para. 2 and 239, UAGCL.

that the goods shall correspond with the description. In case of both sales by sample and by description, it is not sufficient that the bulk corresponds with the sample if the goods do not also correspond with the description.[196] In practice, if a cloth is provided as a sample and is described on the label as 100% cotton, then it should be exactly that. This was the issue in Privy Council case of *Boshali v. Allied Commercial Exported Ltd*[197] which involved a sale by sample and sale by description. Similarly, when buying meat, if it is described as fresh meat, then it should not have previously been frozen.

Because conformity of the goods to the sample and the passing of risk occur at the same time, any damage occurring after that point will be borne by the buyer. If the goods get damaged while in transit therefore and such damage is due to inadequate packaging by the seller, such a situation will be treated as non-conformity already existing during the passing of the risk.[198] This is so because the transfer of title to goods shifts the risk of loss. The seller will therefore be liable for breach of non-conformity.[199]

Examination or Inspection of Goods

Examination or inspection of goods may be performed both during production phase and at the time the goods are put on sale. In both cases, the purpose of examination or inspection is to establish whether the goods conform to the regulations of contractual provisions as regards quality. Regulations requiring the compulsory inspection of quality provide that producers are obliged to observe regulations concerning protection of life, health care and the environment.

As for regulation concerning sale of goods of manufactured goods, the OHADA Uniform At makes provision for the commercial buyer to examine the goods, which seems to be more of a right than an obligation. In fact, the buyer examines the goods before accepting them so that, in the event of their not conforming to the contract, he may give notice to the seller of this fact. Thus, by regulatory control, society has put the buyer in a position in which he cannot avail himself of his rights unless the inspection has first been carried out. Such a business practice today, clearly supports the maim "*caveat emptor*", buyer beware which has gradually proven the weakness of

196 SGA 1893 s 13.
197 [1961] All N.L.R. 946; this case was about "Quality AS 1,000 grey cloth".
198 Articles 256 (upon delivery); 275 (taking delivery shifts title) and 277 para.1 UAGCL.
199 Article 255 UAGCL.

the old maim "*caveat venditor*", seller beware.[200]

The parties may agree that a control of the quality and condition of the goods be carried out by a "third party" who will then issue a certificate concerning their quality and condition. This type of control is used in particular in international trade and has advantages over methods in that the buyer, before receiving the goods, obtains information regarding their condition and may further dispose of them on the basis of the certificate issued by the organisation carrying out the inspection.

Among the many questions and problems arising in connection with the inspection of the goods, the following seem to occur most often: Can the buyer rely on the seller's quality certificate, as provided by some laws? Can the inspection conducted by the buyer effectively reveal certain hidden defects of some types of sophisticated goods? However, regardless of these and a range of other problems encountered by the parties, it should be stressed that quality inspection has been given an extraordinarily important place recently in Cameroon due to her porous borders with other countries within the CEMAC community where they has been a high rate influx of illegal products into the markets. Furthermore, the incessant outcry of local consumers buyers of goods complaining about the low quality of goods stand to corroborate this acute problem. Quality inspection has also taken a considerable importance today because the economy is constantly affected by advanced technological production of goods without which modern trade cannot even be imagined.

Examination of Goods by the Parties to the Contract

Under the UAGCL effective notification of non-conformity depends on two requirements; the content of the notice and the timing of such notice. These two elements represent an extremely important concern because the failure of either one can preclude a buyer from claiming against the effects of non-conformity, even when non-conformity exists.[201] Overall, the Uniform Act imposes relatively stricter requirements upon buyer who examines the goods with a view to ascertaining its state and functionality.

[200] Roland Djieufack & Irene Fokum Sama-lang, "From *Caveat Emptor* to *Caveat Venditor*- An Assessment of Conformity of Goods to the Contract of Sale under the Uniform Act on General Commercial Law: A Contract Law Perspective", (*International Journal of Law and Policy Review [IJLPR]*).

[201] Article 257 UAGCL.

As for the sale of goods (to which compulsory regulations do not apply), the Uniform Act makes provision for the buyer to examine the goods. This seems to be a right. In other words, this is a domain where the contracting parties are free to make their own contractual provision regarding the inspection of the goods, if they wish to. As a rule, however, the buyer usually inspects the goods before accepting them so that, in the event that they do not conform to the contract specification, he may give notice of it to the seller. Thus, the law has put the buyer in a position in which he cannot avail himself of his rights unless the inspection has been carried out in the first place. This is understandable as safety in trade is ensured by such means.

Among the many questions and problems arising in connection with the examination of the goods, the following seem to occur most often: should the inspection of the quality of the goods come first or should the buyer first effect payment? Is it more convenient for the buyer to inspect the goods at the time of dispatch or on arrival? Can the buyer rely on the seller's quality certificate, as provided by some laws? What happens when 'random tests' prove that the goods conform to the quality required and later on it is established that the goods do not conform to the contract? However, regardless of these and a range of other problems encountered by the parties, the courts and arbitrators, it should be stressed that quality inspection has been given an extraordinary important place recently, particularly in view of technical and technological development, and also because it is constantly developing toward specialised activities without which modern trade cannot even be imagined.

Examination by the Seller

The *raison d'être* for the application of Article 255 UAGCL is that a buyer ought to be able to rely on what the parties have agreed. Therefore, the starting point is an assumption by the buyer that the seller will make good any defects if there is any discrepancy between the contract specification and the goods inspected. The presumptive rule in Article 255 UAGCL therefore is that it is the seller who must first show that the parties have agreed that the goods shall have a quality different from that stated in the agreement; in other words, the fact that the buyer knew of or could not have been unaware of the defect, and those parts of the agreement which conflict with this cannot be relied on by the buyer. In any event, Article 255 of the Uniform Act protects the buyer. The buyer is entitled to expect that the goods will conform to the agreement, in practice the written agreement, and that any variance from what should apply under the agreement and under Article 255 para. 1 will be made good by the seller prior to delivering the goods to the buyer. This applies regardless of whether the buyer knows of a defect, if it is agreed that the seller shall deliver the goods without defects.[202]At this point, the parties must be assumed to have expressed their intention in their written agreement in relation to the requirements for the goods in question. By interpretation, Article 255 para. 1 of the Uniform Act seems to restrict application of the *caveat emptor* principle.

Control of quality may also be conducted by the seller, in which case its quality certificate is attached to other documents (which is significant in respect of certain goods since quality may be considerably affected during transportation by reason of environmental considerations and other circumstances). This method of inspection is provided by some governmental or international bodies. The certificate of inspection is the only proof of what it is bound to furnish under the contract. There is, however, another view to the effect that the other party is always entitled to a further inspection.

Examination by the Buyer

As mentioned in the introduction of this chapter, inspection by the buyer is not binding upon him for if he fails to inspect the goods he will incur no sanctions. Therefore, this matter is dealt with by some laws, such as those of the Anglo-Saxon countries, not as being an obligation of the buyer but rather a right.

Under the UAGCL,[203] it is the duty of the buyer obligation to examine the goods or have them examined. Therefore, the law grants an opportunity to the buyer to inspect the goods and report immediately to the seller whether or not they correspond to the contractual description as agreed upon with the seller.[204] The reason behind this exercise may be that, this is duty is stipulated not only in the interest of the seller but also in that of the buyer himself. This duty may be justified first by the need to obtain a clear situation, for by sending the goods to the buyer the seller is put in an uncertain position which cannot last forever. He must know the fate of the goods.

---

[202] René Franz Henschel, "Conformity of Goods in International Sales Governed by CISG Article 35: Caveat Venditor, Caveat Emptor and Contract Law as Background Law and as a Comparing Set of Rules", *Op. cit.*, p. 10.

[203] Article 258 UAGCL.

[204] Akuété Pedro Santos & Jean Yado Toé, *OHADA Droit Commercial Général, Op. cit.*, p. 405.

Although the law does not provide any sanction for the buyer if he fails to perform this duty or fails to report any defect on the goods, he nevertheless loses all his right of action to non conformity of the goods to the contract of sale.[205]Moreover, the buyer losses the same right of action if he fails to notify any defect within a time frame from the time he noticed or ought to have noticed it the defect.[206] That is, depending on the circumstances, the examination of the goods shall be carried out immediately a after he takes delivery to enable the parties determine whether or not the goods are in accordance with the contractual description.[207]

The examination of the goods may be done either by the buyer himself or a third party appointed by him. But he remains the sole person responsible for the performance of that duty even if it is carried out by some other person.[208] Like the CISG, the UAGCL is very clear on this point when it provides that the buyer must examine the goods.[209] However, if an examination is carelessly carried out by a third party duly appointed by him and who does not discover the defect, the buyer is responsible under the contract even though he can institute an action against the appointed examiner.

The basic rule is that examination of the goods is always carried out at the place of delivery, unless the places of delivery and destination are one and the same place. However, the places differ the question that comes up is which of the two should have priority. All depends, of course, on the intention of the parties to the contract and on what they have agreed upon in this regard. For the buyer, however, the place of dispatch may have a number of disadvantages. No matter what the condition of the goods is at the time of loading, it is important for the buyer that they reach him in good condition. It is important for him and therefore to insist that the place of inspection should be at the destination. The presence of the buyer or his representative during inspection at the place of dispatch may incur considerable expense[210], and for this reason, except when this is in the buyer's interest, the latter would rather have the goods inspected at the place of destination.

In some instances, contractual agreements spell out the method to be used to examine the goods.[211] For some industrial engines, for instance,

[205] *Ibid.*.

[206] *Ibid.*.

[207] Articles 258–259 UAGCL.

[208] Article 258 UAGCL.

[209] *Ibid.*.

[210] The reason for this may be that only financially strong buyers will agree to inspection at the place of dispatch. See Jacques Ghestin, Conformité et Garanties dans la Vente (produits mobiliers), *Op. cit.*, pp.263–272.

[211] Case of commodities contracts.

the methods of examining the goods are usually prescribed in the notice guide (hand book). However, where there is no express stipulation on the examination process, the law requires the buyer to rely on common practice, custom and usages for the examination of the goods in question. If neither of the two alternatives is plausible, then a reasonable approach should be used to have the goods thoroughly inspected. What amounts to "reasonable" approach depends on the fact of each case. It does not necessarily mean that the method to be used should be the most sophisticated or costly. What matters is that the buyer should take all necessary steps to have the goods inspected.

As a general rule at Common law,, when the buyer or a third party acting on his behalf examines the goods, such examination is that of the buyer. If carried out, the implied condition as to the defect which such examination ought to have revealed will not be applied.[212]

The examination shall be an objective one, as opposed to the subjective test and any attempt to examine the goods in anyway will merely jeopardise the buyer's right to benefit from the implied condition as to the defect of the goods if they are defective. In other words, a lazy buyer who does not care to examine the goods is more protected than one who did examine only casually.[213]

In the West African Court of Appeal decision's in *Khalil and Dibo v. Mastronikolis*[214] there was no evidence that the oil was not of merchantable quality when the agent of the buyer examined the outside of the drums of the oil and took the sample. The leading Common law authority in this case, most often referred to by courts (of Common law jurisdiction) in Arica is the case of *Thornett and Febr v. Beers and Sons.*[215] With a fact of the case similar to the *Khalil and Dibo's case, Bary, J. in Thornett and Febr's case* held that there was no implied condition to be observed as the buyer was given opportunity to examine the goods, which he did. The buyer in this case, carried out examination of the outside of some barrels of glue; he did not go through a thorough examination though he had been given opportunity and facilities to do so. Taking into account case law and statutory position, it appears that what matters is not the mere opportunity given for examination but the proper examination itself.

---

212 P.S. Atiyah et al., *The Sale of Goods, Op. cit.*, p .182.
213 *Ibid.*, pp.171–172.
214 [1949] 12 WACA 462.
215 [1919] 1K.B 486.

However, Common law and statutory positions have not in these circumstances explained what exactly amounts to examination, when there is examination and what it entails. Even as concerns the sale by sample, the buyer should be given a reasonable opportunity to compare the bulk with the sample.[216] It may be inferred from trade practice that comparison may imply examination of the goods. In the SGA, this is a mere restatement of buyer's right to examine the goods supplied before acceptance.[217] In the case of *Lorymer v. Smit*,[218] it was held that the buyer of the consignment of wheat by sample has the inalienable right to inspect the whole in bulk at any proper and convenient time and that in case the seller refuses to show it, the buyer may rescind the whole contract. In other words, common law makes it clear that, once the buyer inspects and compares the sample, he cannot complain later of any defect in the bulk which a reasonable examination ought to have revealed.[219]

However, what amounts to reasonable examination was determined in the case of *Godley v. Perry*.[220] It was held that practical examination of the goods does not constitute reasonable examination. In this case, when the child bought a toy catapult after seeing a sample on the window, the examination was carried out pulling back its elastic. Later on, in using the toy, the plastic got cut and injured the child on his eye. It was held that the seller was in breach of a contract of sale[221] as the defect that caused harm to the child was not apparent and his inspection as a buyer was all that a reasonable purchaser could have done. But whenever the buyer examines the goods and does in fact discovers the defect, but decides to take the goods all the same, if the defect in the sample turns the goods unmerchantable, whether or not the buyer has knowledge of that fact, he has no ground to complaint at all.[222]

Method of Examination

The Uniform Act is silent as to the methods of examining the goods by the buyer. Methods of examination are determined either by the contract or in accordance with the laws and customs of the place where the inspection is carried out. What is legally relevant in connection with the method of

[216] SGA 1893 s 15 (2) (b).
[217] SGA 1893 s 34.
[218] 1822] 1^{B} & C 1.
[219] *Moody v. Gregson* [1868] LR Ex 49.
[220] Supra.
[221] SGA 1893 s 17 (2) .
[222] Igweike K.I., *Sales of Goods, Nigerian Commercial Law, Op. cit.*, pp. 82–83.

examination is that any method of inspection is allowed (as per the intention of the parties) which will enable ascertainment of the quality of goods. The fact that one method of inspection is stipulated in the contract and another applied is of no importance. As a matter of fact, there are various methods of quality inspection and among them the most frequent are expert examination, comparison with the sample or by the condition in which the goods are sold.

Examination by Sample

The type of examination required also depends on the circumstances of each case and the kind of goods in question: thus agricultural products would usually be inspected by comparison with the sample whilst the control of automobiles and machinery necessitates a very complex expert analysis (comparison with specifications, technical conditions, etc.)

When generic goods are sold examination by sample is normally sufficient- and also required within a very short time after delivery: the buyer is deemed to have been able to find out the defects on delivery if they are easily discoverable. The inspection may be total or partial, and which of the two will be undertaken does not depend on the will of the parties but on the kind of the goods in question. A full control of bulbs, for example, would mean destruction of the product. However, there are products which necessitate a complete inspection (particularly when their use and application are connected with human safety).

Hence, it is understandable why the Uniform Act regulating the question of quality of goods provide that the seller shall deliver goods of the same quality as the sample.[223] Consequently, it is a duty of the buyer to ascertain the quality and character of the goods delivered in comparison with the sample which was presented to him by the buyer during the formation of the contract.

The SGA gives the buyer the right to examine the goods at delivery if they have not previously been examined. The buyer is not deemed to have accepted them unless and until he has a reasonable opportunity of examining them for the purpose of ascertaining whether they are in conformity with the contract.[224]

[223] Article 255 para. 2 UAGCL.

[224] SGA 1893 s 34.

In most cases, where the buyer is entitled to reject the goods due to the non-conformity or when the contract is subject to some condition express or implied as to quality[225] or otherwise with the contract of sale, as the case particularly with contract for sale by sample[226] or by description,[227] the position is similar; the buyer is given the reasonable opportunity to examine the goods otherwise he is not deemed to have accepted the them.

Still under the SGA, there is an implied condition that the buyer shall have a reasonable opportunity of comparing the bulk with the sample.[228] Under a contract for sale by description, whether the seller of these goods is a manufacturer or not, there is an implied condition that the goods shall be of good quality; provided that if the buyer has examined the goods, there is no implied condition as regards defects which such examination ought to have revealed.[229]

Examination as to the Condition in which the Goods are Sold

It is not certain that an opportunity to inspect goods conditioned in certain form such as packaging, frozen goods, or can foods will reveal true facts about the goods. The question is thus a double one: is a seller or retailer who sells food products in the ordinary tin can or other sealed container responsible for injury caused to his customers either from some foreign article in the can or from unwholesomeness of the food; and second, is the seller who sells the food products in bulk, which are defective in some way for which the retailer cannot reasonably be held at fault liable for injuries resulting to his customers from the defect?[230] It is therefore understandable why the Uniform Act regulating the quality of goods provides that the seller shall be liable to deliver the goods "in the usual manner" the goods are packaged.[231] This suggests that the buyer is liable to inspect the goods in conformity with the usual method in which such goods are packaged. In this condition, the warranty will have to be implied although the buyer has made complete examination of the product on the basis of the seller's ability to judge and having knowledge of the goods which he has been dealing for long.

225 A breach of warrantee does not give rise to the rejection of the goods.
226 SGA 1893 s 15 (2) (c).
227 SGA 1893 s 14 (2).
228 SGA 1893, s 13 (1).
229 SGA 1893 s 16 (2).
230 Robert C. Brown, "The Liability of Retail Dedalers for Defective Food Products", *Op. cit.*
231 Article 255 para. 2 UAGCL.

This may be justified by the fact it is sometimes not possible for the buyer to detect inherent latent defects of goods which are sealed or packaged since the buyer has just the immediate opportunity to appreciate the goods from their appearance.

There is a strong line of authority in favour of holding the seller who is dealer in such products in a sealed container liable for from injuries resulting from the unwholesomeness of the food or some foreign substance in the can. Suffice it to say at this point that a retailer should not be exempted from liability based on the tort of negligence.

There are a number of problems which are closely connected with the problem now under consideration- that is, the liability of the seller-the dealer of such packaged products. The fundamental reason for the extreme liability with respect to sales of such products (especially sales of food) is the necessity for the protection of public health and safety. The OHADA laws on conformity should be extended to such articles where there is substantial degree of injury not particularly personal but detrimental to the buyer's business in that economic loss may be incurred. Yet the OHADA Uniform Act does not seem to have gone far. Certainly, it has not imposed rigid liability for personal injury because the whole provisions on warranty under the Uniform Act are actionable under contract law. It appears to fall under the domain of consumer law since the Uniform Act on General Commercial Law does not cover goods for personal consumption or use.[232] The same argument, however, may be made in regard to any implied warranty, not only for food, but of other articles where the seller could not discover the defect. There is strong reason for holding the seller liable for selling defective can food than in any other kind of sale.[233]

It may then be conceded that the argument in favour of exempting the dealer under such circumstances from liability is not entirely foreclosed by the terms of the UAGCL; but it seems clear that the Act neither does nor was intended to make any special provision for this situation, and that under the general rules laid down by the Uniform Act, a warranty of fitness for the purpose and merchantability may be applied. It seems rather obvious that in this situation, the present rule is and ought to be *caveat venditor—let the seller beware.*

---

[232] Article 235 (a) UAGCL.

[233] see Rollin M. Pekins, "Unwholesome Food as a Source of Liability", (1919–1920) 5 *Iowa L. Bull.* 6, pp. 86–111.

Eamination by the Seller

Although in practice the goods are usually inspected by the buyer, there are situations where the examination made by the seller will be the only inspection. This will be the case when the contracting parties so agree, that is, if such inspection is "in the interest of both contracting parties". It is often impractical (or expensive) for the buyer to attend the inspection at the time of loading, and in such cases the parties may agree that the seller himself shall inspect the goods. In the case of sales at a distance at the time of delivery of the goods to the carrier, the seller is obliged to inspect the goods before forwarding them to the buyer along with the necessary supporting documents as to their quality.[234]

Inspection by Third Parties

As mentioned above, the inspection may be carried out by the parties (usually the buyer) and many problems may arise in this connection, the most important of which is when an allegation is made that the party who inspected the goods has not been impartial. On the other hand, with trade at a distance it may be far too expensive for the buyer to send his representative to the place of inspection of the goods, for which reason (and often due to insufficient expertise) the buyer (and sometimes the seller, as well) enter with into a separate contract with a "third party" who is to inspect the goods and send the report on the findings. This is the purport of Article 270 of the UAGCL. The "third party" may be an individual or (more commonly) a private organisation specialised in providing this type of service.

Time for Examination

As to the time of the examination, of the goods, there is a generally accepted view that it should be done "immediately", "without delay", "as soon as (conveniently) possible". It should be stressed here that in interpreting these expressions attention should be paid to the circumstances of each case and that the time be limited to what is normal in the trade in that particular kind of goods. These are of course factual questions and a significant role played here by the commercial customs of each branch of trade.

[234] Article 250 UAGCL.

The UAGCL suggests no more than a short period within which the examination of the goods should be carried out, if necessary, as quickly as possible.[235] Unlike in the former UAGCL, there now exist a prescribed time period for the buyer to conduct examination of the goods as governed by the amended UAGCL. The time preceding this process determines the end of the inspection and it is immaterial whether or not the goods conform to the terms of the contract. Henceforth, the question to be answered is when in fact the inspection or examination starts and ends.

The UAGCL provides that the examination of the goods starts upon delivery or one month following delivery,[236] or sometimes depending on the circumstances, the time may be different from the delivery time particularly when the goods are in transit or when they are redirected, deviated or re-dispatched.[237]

The examination of the goods at delivery may sometimes be delayed when the contract requires the transportation of the goods. This certainly occurs in many international contracts of sale of goods where the goods have to be handed over to a carrier. This position is dealt with under the UAGCL when it provides that the examination will take place once the goods reach destination.[238] Also, unlike the general rule, the time of examination of the goods will be when they reach their new destination. In this case, the UAGCL allows for a period of one year for the buyer to report any latent defect from the time the defect is discovered. This solution applies when the goods have been re-dispatched, deviated or redirected by the buyer without him having the chance them. However, this solution will not only apply if the buyer, at the time of the conclusion of the contract, knew or ought to have known of the possibility of such deviation or re-dispatching.[239] In practice, a buyer operating as a middleman or a buyer who intends to sell is presumed to be aware of either the redirection or deviation. In this case, practice sometimes requires such a buyer to inform the seller beforehand.

---

[235] Articles 258, 259 and 270 para. 1 UAGCL. The predecessor of this was Article 227 (1) of the old version of the UAGCL.

[236] Articles 256 and 258, UAGCL.

[237] Article 270 para. 2 UAGCL.

[238] Article 270 para. 2 UAGCL.

[239] Article 259 UAGCL.

Notice Requirement

As to the content of a notice of non-conformity, under the CISG such notice must be sufficiently specific regarding the "nature of the lack of conformity" in order for the buyer to meet up with his business needs. Sufficiency in this respect is determined by the purpose of the notice in mind. As one commentator has suggested, [q]uestions as to what the notice should be answered with regard to the functions served by the notice . . . [and] the principal functions [under the CISG] are to give the seller an opportunity to obtain and preserve evidence of the condition of the goods and to cure the deficiency.[240]

The UAGCL provides two instances where the buyer should give notice to the seller for any lack of conformity of the goods being delivered: the buyer must give notice of a lack of conformity discovered one month after the day of delivery.[241] Failure to observe these requirements, the buyer will be deprived of his right to claim redress of the non-conformity. Secondly, the buyer must give notice of any hidden defect of conformity within one year from the moment when this was discovered or ought to be known.[242] To this effect, notice is therefore necessary in order to exercise all remedies available to the buyer under the Uniform Act.[243]

There is no requirement as to a specific form of notice under the Uniform Act. Notice need not be written;[244] it may be given by word of mouth, for example by telephone. This problem in the latter case is of course evidence. Pursuant to Article 240 UAGCL, the buyer can prove it simply by all possible means.

Time Limits (Prescription) for Giving Notice

The question of time limit to the buyer's action must be clearly distinguished from the one addressed in Article 259 UAGCL, where the cut-off period of one year to give notice of non-conformity is provided. The period to give notice runs from the moment the buyer either discovered or ought to have

240 John O. Honnold, Uniform Law for International Sales, *Op. cit.*, p. 277–278.
241 Article 257 UAGCL.
242 Article259 UAGCL; under the CISG, the time frame is (2 years) Article 39 CISG.
243 Articles 282, 283 and 284 UAGCL.
244 The word 'written' shall mean any communication using a written medium, including the telegram, telex, telefax or e-mail .

discovered the lack of conformity.[245]

Before he examines the goods, someone may inform the buyer of the lack of conformity. In this case, the time of giving notice begins to run at the moment the buyer acquired this knowledge. It is therefore immaterial whether or not he had examined the goods.

Prescription concerns legal actions and bars a claim even if the buyer did give notice. Conversely, a longer time limit for an action does not influence the cut-off period of Article 259 UAGCL. In theory, the buyer would still be able to lay his claim, but he cannot rely on a lack of conformity if he has not given notice within one year of delivery. Parties may derogate to the latter rule by stipulating a different period of guarantee.

It is important to the seller that notice is not only timely, but also sufficiently specific as to the goods concerned and the nature of the defect. It has been stated by a writer that even if the buyer has bought a single item of a certain kind from the seller, he must give notice referring not only to the type of goods, but also to the specific item in question (serial number, date of delivery), in order for the seller to identify with precision the allegedly defective goods without having to read all sales documents or to gather information.[246]

As in the CISG, the period of time in the UAGCL related to the report on the notice of conformity[247] is independent but additional to the period of the examination of the goods.[248] In other words, nothing prevents the buyer from examining the goods in spite of the cut-off period of one year. Although the two durations may appear similar, the clear distinction between them lies on the fact that the buyer will lose his right to rely on the lack of conformity, unless the one time period has expired.[249] The buyer up to that period has the right to continue with the examination of the goods, which may reveal some immediate true facts of the goods before a period of one year. It follows therefore that in determining what amount to "one year" as the duration for giving notice will depend on the facts of each case. Most often regard is made as to whether the goods are seasonal or perishable, or whether the goods require an additional expert opinion. Hence, depending on each particular case, the time to give notice is defined.[250]

245 Article 258 UAGCL.
246 Anna Veneziano,"Non-Conformity of Goods in International Sales; A Survey of Current Caselaw on CISG", *Op. cit.*, p.52.
247 *Ibid.*, UAGCL; Article 39(1) CISG.
248 Article 257 UAGCL; Article 38 CISG.
249 Articles 258–259 UAGCL.
250 Ingebord Schwenzer, *Op. cit.*, p. 630.

As a general rule, the "1 year" time limit to give notice runs from the moment the goods are handed over to the buyer.[251] Thereafter, the time limit elapses and the buyer loses all rights to rely on the lack of conformity. It is irrelevant and immaterial whether or not the buyer could not have knowledge of it or it was impossible to discover the lack of conformity.[252] The seller is therefore free from any lack of conformity claim after the time limit has elapsed. However, one year time limit remains a default rule. The UAGCL makes it clear that parties are free to determine their time limit for notice.[253] It therefore appears that parties can either exclude or modify this limitation period but the seller still has the obligation to perform his duties as contained in Article 255 regarding the quality of the goods.

Once the buyer fails to observe the notice requirement as provided by the law, he immediately losses all rights to rely on the lack of conformity.[254] It follows that the buyer losses all available remedies[255] he would have been entitled to if he had performed the requirement of notice.[256] In short, he will be solely responsible if the goods happen to be defective.

From the reading of some provisions of the Uniform Act, parties may derogate by agreement from the examination and notice requirements. The case makes it clear that the opportunity of drafting a more complete set of terms on lack of conformity is to be taken into account. One solution might be to distinguish between apparent and hidden defects, providing for a longer period of time under the Uniform Act which is one year period.[257] This leaves the courts the task of interpreting when a lack of conformity is easy to discover. Another option is to leave out any reference to the nature of the non- conformity and provide for a short term starting together with a maximum period guarantee starting from delivery: which is one month under the Uniform Act.[258]

Finally, Articles 258 and 259 of the Uniform Act may be derogated also by usage under Article 238 para. 2 UAGCL. When parties have agreed on a contractual time for notice, however, the applicability of usage is excluded.

---

251 Article 259 UAGCL.
252 Ingebord Schwenzer, *Op. cit.*, p. 637.
253 Article 259 UAGCL.
254 Articles 282, 283 and 284 UAGCL.
255 Articles 282 -284 UAGCL.
256 Articles 258 & 259 UAGCL.
257 259 UAGCL.
258 Article 258 UAGCL.

Conclusion

The concept of conformity in the OHADA Uniform Act on General Commercial Law is an umbrella term which encompasses lots of factors which the commercial buyer may expect. As the seller's material duty of conformity is concerned, it is common for the quality or description of the goods to incorporate some elements that are not part of the physical characteristics of the goods, and such requirements such as Good Manufacturing Practices and ethical values should not be seen as novel. The prime consideration in determining the seller's material obligation of conformity under the Uniform Act is the intention of the parties. The text of the Uniform Act emphasises the need to uphold the intention of the parties, including with reference to any trade usages. The notion of ethical and GMP practices will often form part of these trade usages. Article 255 of the Act is structured to create rules of interpretation rather than that of binding force.

The seller's act in exercising his material duty of conformity is not enough. The seller is also expected to deliver goods which will satisfactorily serve the purpose for which commercial buyers intend to use them. As the seller's duty of conformity is expansive, imposing an absolute liability, it is critical for the buyer to clearly articulate the purpose(s) for which he intends to use the goods which is considered as the seller's functional duty of conformity. This is especially important for manufactured goods, where the quality of the goods is relevant for its saleability by the commercial buyer in view to meet up with consumer expectations. The utility of the goods for re-sale matters for the commercial buyer in the first place. That is why the seller under the UAGCL is under the duty to deliver goods for the required purpose.

The seller's expected obligation to deliver goods satisfying the requirements of the contract would hardly in practice be that. The seller in most cases is not always to be blamed for all lack of conformity. The buyer also has the responsibility to ensure conformity.Thus, since doing business is at the heart of the mind of the commercial buyer, he has been given the opportunity by the OHADA Uniform Act on General Commercial Law to examine the existence of any defect in the goods supplied to him by the seller. This inadequacy takes the form of latent or hidden defects which may be inherent in the goods. This situation seems to show how the principle of *caveat venditor* confronts with the principle of *caveat emptor.* Arguably, this task seems to be difficult with the increment of sophisticated goods being manufactured today. The bare eyes of a buyer cannot detect some deficiency existing in some kinds of goods. Some technical methods need to be employed by the buyer. Time allocation has also been specified for the buyer to report any such lack of conformity to the seller for a possible remedy. The buyer's right to examine the goods could be said to be a contribution in ascertaining the quality of goods in the markets. The commercial buyer cares because his customers are his interest in the re-selling business he operates.

4

THE CONTROL OF PRICES IN THE CAMEROONIAN ECONOMY

Introduction

Formal business laws are important. They do exist in Cameroon, but they are not in evidence in the informal sector, let alone predictably enforced there. There is need to assess the business-law reality regulating price control in the formal and informal sectors before considering how to rectify any lapse.

Considerations Involved in Formulating the Pricing Policy in Cameroon

Economic considerations

The pricing policy in Cameroon varies from firm to firm depending on its objectives. In practice, we find many prices for a product of a firm such as wholesale price, retail price, published price, quoted, actual price and so on. Special discounts, special offers, methods of payment, amounts bought and transportation charges, trade-in values etc are some sources of variations in the price of a product. Pricing decision of a firm in general will have considerable repercussions on its marketing strategies. This implies that when a firm makes a decision about the price, it has to consider its entire marketing efforts. Pricing decisions are usually considered a part of the general strategy for achieving a broadly defined goal. Some of the economic considerations vital in formulating the pricing policy in Cameroon shall be examined in the paragraphs that follow.

Competitive situations

Pricing Policy is to be set in the light of competitive situations in the market. There is the need to know whether the firm is facing perfect or imperfect competition. In perfect competition, the producers have no control on the price. Pricing policy has special significance only under imperfect competition. Again, the business people use the pricing device for the purpose of maximising profits. Generally, business people are reluctant to charge high prices for their products because this might result in bringing more manufacturers and producers into the industry. In most circumstances, firms will want to prevent the entry of rivals. It is for this reason that pricing should take care of the long run welfare of a company.

Flexibility

Pricing policies should be flexible enough to meet changes in economic conditions of various customer industries. If a firm is selling its product in a highly competitive market, it will have very little scope for pricing discretion. Prices should also be flexible to take care of cyclical variations. To this effect, the government may prevent the firms in forming combinations to set a high price. Often the government prefers to control the prices of essential commodities in Cameroon such as cement, roofing sheets, domestic gas, sugar with a view to prevent the exploitation of consumers. The entry of the government into the pricing process tends to inject politics into price fixation by laying down policies and rules as one will find in the 2015 Law on Commercial Activities in Cameroon.

Pricing is not an end in itself but a means to an end. The fundamental guides to pricing, therefore are the firms overall goals. The broadest of them is survival. On a more specific level, objectives relate to rate of growth, market share, maintenance of control and finally profit. The various objectives may not always be compatible. A pricing policy should never be established without consideration as to its impact on the other policies and practice.

Price sensitivity

The various factors which may generate insensitivity to price changes are variability in consumer behaviour, variations in the effectiveness of marketing effort, nature of the product, importance of service after sales etc.

Businessmen often tend to exaggerate the importance of price sensitivity and ignore many identifiable factors which tend to minimise it. Producers and manufacturers in Cameroon may have to take many pricing decisions. If the data on demand and cost are highly conjectural, the firm has to rely on some mechanical formula. If a firm is selling its product in a highly competitive market, it will have very little scope for price discretion. This will have the way for routinised pricing. In setting up a pricing policy of any society, some factors must be used as guide.

Cost Data in Pricing:

Cost Data occupy an important place in the pricing setting process. There are different types of costs incurred in the production and marketing of a product. There are production costs, promotional expenses like advertising or personal selling as well as taxation. These may necessitate an upward fixing of price. For example, the prices of petrol and gas in Cameroon are rising due to rise in the cost of raw materials such as crude oil transportation, refining etc. If costs go up, price rise may be quite justified. However, their relevance to the pricing decision must neither be underestimated nor exaggerated. For setting prices apart from costs, a number of other factors have to be taken into consideration. They are demand and competition.

Costs here are of two types; fixed costs and variable costs. In the short period, that is, the period in which a firm wants to establish itself, the firm may not cover the fixed costs but it must cover the variable costs. In the long run, all costs must be covered. If the entire costs are not covered, the producer stops production. If cost were to determine prices why do so many companies report losses? There are marked differences in cost as between one producer and another. Yet the fact remains that the prices are very close for somewhat similar product. This is a very important evidence of the fact that costs are not the determining factors in pricing.

Price decisions cannot be based merely on cost accounting data which only contribute to history while prices have to work in the future. Again, it is very difficult to measure costs accurately. Costs are affected by volume, and volume is affected by price. To add, the management of any production or manufacturer has to assume some desired price-volume relationship for determining costs. This explains why costs play even a less important role in connection with new products than with the older ones. Until the market is decided and some idea is obtained about volume, it is not possible to determine costs.

Regarding the role of costs in pricing, it has been observed that the cost may be regarded only as an indicator of demand and price. Again, the cost at any given time represents a resistance point to the lowering of price. Costs determine profit margins at various levels of output.

Another question that is often asked is to know what are the relevant costs for pricing decisions? Though in the long run, all cost have to be covered, for managerial decisions in the short run, direct costs are relevant. In a single production firm, the management will try to cover all the costs. In a multi-production firm, problems are more complex. For pricing decision, relevant costs are those costs that are directly traceable to an individual product. Ordinarily, the selling price must cover all direct costs that are attributable to a product. In addition, it must contribute to the common cost and to the realisation of profit. If the price, in the short run is lower than the cost, the question arises, whether this covers the variable cost. If it covers the variable cost, the low price can be accepted. On the other hand, in the long run, the firm cannot sell at a price lower than the cost. Product pricing decision should be lower than the cost. Product pricing decision should therefore be made with a view to maximise company's profits in the long run.

Demand Factor in Pricing

In pricing of a product, demand occupies a very important place. In fact, demand is more important for effective sales. The elasticity of demand is to be recognised in determining the price of the product. If the demand for the product is inelastic, the firm can fix a high price. On the other hand, if the demand is elastic, it has to fix a lower price. In the very short term, the chief influence on price is normally demand. Manufacturers of durable goods always set a high price, even though sales are affected. If the price is too high, it may also affect the demand for the product. They wait for the arrival of a rival product with competitive price. Therefore, demand for product is very sensitive to price changes.

Consumer psychology in pricing:

Demand for a product depends upon the psychology of the consumers. Sensitivity to price change will vary from consumer to consumer. In a particular situation, the behaviour of one individual may not be the same as that of the other. In fact the pricing decision ought to rest on a more incisive rationale than simple elasticity. There are consumers who buy a product provided its quality is high. Generally, product quality, product image, customer service and promotion activities influence many consumers than the price. These factors are qualitative and ambiguous. From the point of view of consumers, prices are quantitative and unambiguous. Price constitutes a barrier to demand when it is too low, just as much as when it is too high.

Above a particular price, the product is regarded as too expensive and below another price, as constituting a risk of not giving adequate values. If the price is too low, consumers will tend to think that a product of inferior quality is being offered. With an improvement in incomes hopefully in Cameroon, the average consumer will become quality conscious. This may lead to an increase in the demand for durable goods. People of high incomes buy products even though their prices are high. In the affluent societies, price is the indicator of quality.

Competitive Factor in Pricing

Market situation plays an important role in pricing. Pricing policy has some managerial discretion where there is a considerable degree of in perfect competition; the individual producers have no discretion in pricing. They have to accept the price fixed by the forced of demand and supply. In monopoly, the producer fixes a high price for his product. In other market situations like oligopoly and monopolistic competition, the individual producers take the prices of the rival products in determining their price. If the primary determinant of price changes the competitive condition in the market price, the pricing policy can least be categorised as competition based pricing.

Profit Factor in Pricing:

In fixing the price for products, the producers consider mainly the profit aspect. Each producer has his aim of profit maximisation. If the objective is profit maximisation, the critical role is to select a price at which MR=MC. Generally, the pricing policy is based on the goal of obtaining a reasonable profit. Most of the business people will want to hold the price at constant level. They do not desire constant price fluctuations. The profit maximisation approach to price setting is logical because it forces decision markers to focus their attention on the changes in production, cost, revenue and profit associated with any contemplated change in price. The price rigidity is the practice of many producers. Rigidity does not mean inflexibility. It means that prices are stable over a given period.

Leaving the producer and or wholesalers and retailers of goods and services as examined under the various heads above, to determine the price that will be generally accepted at all levels in Cameroon, citizens stand the chance of suffering from indiscriminate pricing and it is for this reason the legislature in Cameroon through the 2015 Law on Commercial Activity in Cameroon has outlined provisions guaranteeing or safeguarding a fair pricing policy to ensure a fairer play ground.

Legal Considerations

The 2015 Law in Cameroon has laid down some conditions pertaining to the sale of products and services and prices, but for the sake of this work, emphasis shall be placed on prices.[259]

In Cameroon, the law mentioned above guarantees that prices of goods and rates of services should be freely determined through a healthy and fair market competition. However, the determination of the prices and rates of some sensitive products and services, particularly basic necessities or monopolies, may be subject to the prior approval procedure, according to the conditions and procedure laid down by regulation.[260] Equally, the list of goods and services whose prices and rates are subject to the prior approval procedure should be prepared by order of the Minister in charge of Trade. Decisions relating to the prices and rates of some products and services have to be made by order of the Minister in charge of Trade, who may equally delegate authority to Regional Governors or approved public bodies. The prices and rates of some products and services may also be fixed through consultation between the Ministry in charge of Trade and various sector operators. The memorandum of understanding resulting from such consultations shall have authority by order of Minister in charge of prices.[261] The ministry in charge of prices may also by order, oblige the prior filing of the pricing and rate schedules of some staple products and services.[262]

Any sale of goods or provision of service that does not fall under free pricing has to be done in compliance with regulated, approved or coordinated

[259] see part II of chapter III on the 2015 Law governing commercial activity in Cameroon on prices.

[260] Section 44 (1).

[261] see section 44 (4)

[262] *Ibid.* (5)

prices, as the case may be, in accordance with the regulation in force.[263] Every vendor or service provider has as an obligation to equally inform customers about prices, tariffs and conditions of sale of goods and services and the vendor or service provider shall by means of labelling, display or by any other appropriate procedure, inform the consumer on the prices and tariffs of the goods and services. Prices and rates on the domestic market have to be indicated in local currency and not in foreign currencies, in an unequivocal, easily visible and clearly legible manner. All taxes corresponding to the total amount payable by the customer to purchase a good or service have to be indicated.

The traders of alcohol and non-alcoholic beverage establishments, accommodation facilities, restaurants and consumers trade shows shall indicate prices, inclusive of service charges and where reference is made of the sale price of a product or service in a commercial advertisement, the price has to be indicated in accordance with section 46 of the 2015 Law.[264]It should be equally said here that the special conditions governing information on prices applicable to some activity sectors or specific goods and services can only be laid down by law or regulation and unless otherwise provided in the general terms and conditions of sale or agreed upon between the parties, the prices of goods sold and services provided by any trader shall be deemed to be payable in cash during the sale or on the date and place of delivery or removal.

Payment may, by agreement between the parties, be postponed to a later date following delivery or removal. Payment under no circumstances should take place before the sale is concluded. Clearance sales shall be preceded by announcement indicating notably;

— the price reduction margin in absolute terms;
— goods or services, categories of the goods or services concerned;
— conditions under which the advantages announced are granted, particularly the period during which the product or service is provided at a discount.

The labelling, marking or display of prices shall show, besides the reduced price, the reference or previous price. All goods or services ordered during the period to which a price reduction advertisement relates must be delivered or sold at the price indicated in the advertisement and no advertisement of

263 Section 45
264 *Ibid.*

price or discount may be made on items that are not available for sale or on services that cannot be provided during the period announced.[265] It is against this back drop that the government of Cameroon has resorted to the control of prices.

Formal business laws technically applicable on price controls in the formal sector

Just as formal business law exists in Cameroon, so does formal price law. The discussion starts with the 2015 law regulating commercial activities in Cameroon because it applies to transactions between the supplier and the retail seller. The control of prices of products and services in Cameroon is an additional safe guard put in place by the Ministry of Trade that is in charge of prices. This control is done by authorised administrative authorities of the Ministry duly recognised and supported by Law. It is equally government's intervention and whose activity is carried out at least twice a year in all the markets and shops all over the national territory. These authorities from the Ministry carry out control of prices from manufacturers through wholesalers and to retailers. Government gains favour with voters and constituents when it lowers the price of popular goods. Government also gains favor from lobbyists and firms when it raises prices to promote the health of the industry. Price controls can take the form of maximum[266] and minimum[267] prices. They are a way to regulate prices and set either above or below the market equilibrium. Maximum prices can reduce the price of food to make it more affordable, but the drawback is that a maximum price may lead to lower supply and a shortage. Minimum prices can increase the price producers receive. They have been used in agriculture to increase farmers' income. However, minimum prices lead to over-supply.

One of the reasons that governments like that of Cameroon invoke price controls is to ensure that goods and services are sold at a 'fair' price. In a situation with numerous well-informed consumers purchasing from

[265] see entirely section 49 of the 2015 Law.

[266] A maximum price means firms are not allowed to set prices above a certain level. The aim is to reduce prices below the market equilibrium price. The advantage is that it may lead to lower prices for consumers. This may be important if the supplier has monopoly power to exploit consumers. Maximum prices are a method to bring prices closer to a 'fair' and 'competitive equilibrium.

[267] Minimum prices are used to give producers a higher income. For example, they are used to increase the income of farmers producing food.

multiple sellers who can develop a reputation for high or low quality, the free market works well. The market price is 'fair' due to the competition between innovators and between buyers. However, there are occasions when entrants are discouraged or the information available to one or more parties is poor. In such cases, government may impose price controls in an effort to protect citizens from exploitation.

More typically, the government of Cameroon tries to fix the bad effects of price controls with subsidies to the low supplied activity. In the case of the pharmaceutical industry, these subsidies go to research and development. A subsidy could restore the free market outcome by lowering the cost of research. Again, however, the difficulty arises in choosing the level of the subsidy, deciding whether and how to award it to for-profit corporations, and avoiding inefficient lobbying and corruption. In practice, these are very difficult issues to manage in a way that benefits consumers. With these controls[268] from the government, some manufacturers and business people hold that a free pricing system is better.

The pricing system in the informal sector: The case of used -goods

The informal sector is important to Sub-Saharan Africa. Much of this region's economy, including that of the seventeen OHADA member-states, is part of the informal sector. The informal sector produces 30% of worldwide GDP,[269] and conservatively between 40% and 60% of the Sub-Saharan economy.[270] In Cameroon, it is estimated that the informal sector generated approximately 42% of GDP in 1995-96.The informal sector is sometimes defined as the part of a national economy that is not represented in the GDP.[271] Although informal-sector activity is not necessarily illegal, this definition includes tax evasion, as well as the operation of illegal businesses.[15]

[268] For more on the problems of price control in general, see Fiona M. Scott Morton in his article *the Cato Review of Business and Government.(Vol. 24, No. 1, 2001).*

[269] U.N. Dev. Programme, Comm'n on Legal Empowerment of the Poor, 1 Making the Law Work for Everyone 15 (2008), available at http:// der.oas.org/Institutional_relations/ Final%20Report_English.pdf.

[270] See Friedrich Schneider & Dominik H. Enste, Shadow Economies: Size, Causes, and Consequences, 38 *J. Econ. Lit.* 77, 78-79 (2000).

[271] see generally Claire Moore Dickerson, Informal-Sector Entrepreneurs, Development and Formal Law: A Functional Understanding of Business Law, 59 Am. J. Comp. L. 179, 185 (2011); Fone Anne Marie,(1998) "Le Secteur Informel Camerounais au regard du Doit Commercial", Tome 2, *Annales de la Facultés des Sciences Juridiques,* Université de Dschang ; Noel Thierry Kanchop, *Le Secteur Informel a l'Epreuve du Droit des Affaires OHADA,* Mémoire de D.E.A., Université de Dschang, 2008.

The definition of the informal sector is complicated by the permeable nature of its border with the formal sector. Many workers in the formal sector also work in the informal sector. For example, a fully licensed restaurant owner may operate a dress-and-accessories shop out of a back room. A hairdresser may have an official shop, but also cut and style hair from home or go to clients' homes. A dress-shop owner may well have a second, unofficial location at home. Indeed, a tailor who works exclusively in a particular shop may still have a part of the business in the informal sector. Because the border is so porous, it is difficult to identify which activities are in that sector. Nevertheless, the small size of the interviewees' businesses and the relatively mechanical types of taxes they paid together increased their ability to fly under the government's information-gathering radar. This helps characterize them as informal-sector entrepreneurs.

In fact, price control began in Cameroon, with Law no. 63/LF/27, of the 19th June 1963, which established a regime of price control.

The substantial provisions on price control in the country consist essentially in placing goods under three different categories, and in attributing to each category a particular method of determining prices.[272] These categories are (a) essential goods (such as foodstuffs and other necessaries), (b) heavy and bulky goods (building materials, for example), and (c) luxury goods (jewellery for instance). Different profit margins are allowed to the sellers of these goods. The base-line for the determination of the profit margins is the gross cost of the goods in question, in the case of imported goods, their cost, insurance, freight and other warehouse and transport charges, and in the case of home-produced goods, the manufacturers' or producers' prices.[273] Furthermore, different profit margins apply depending on whether the seller is a wholesaler or retailer.[274]

In addition to these general provisions, specific legislation has been enacted to deal with particular businesses. Ministerial Order No. 14/MINEP/DPPM, of March 4 regulates the sales of pharmaceutical products. Another Order, No. 006/MINDIC/DC/82 which deals with activities related to the automobile industry.

In spite of the above facts, price controls presents some demerits. The imposition of price controls on a well-functioning, competitive market harms

[272] Arrêté no. 0196/MINCOMMERCE du 13 April 2007 portant fixation de la liste des produits et services dont les prix et tarifs sont soumis a la procédure d'homologation préalable.

[273] Arrêté no. 100/MINDIC/DPPM du 12 Décembre 1988 fixant les éléments constitutifs du prix de revient et les marges bénéficiaires applicable aux produits importés, aux produits de fabrication locale et aux prestations de services.

[274] Details are spelt out in Decree No. 69/DF/409 of October 2nd 1969.

society by reducing the amount of trade in the economy and creating incentives to waste resources. Many researchers have found that price controls reduce entry and investment in the long run. The controls can also reduce quality, create black markets, and stimulate costly rationing. In the case of pharmaceuticals, the most damaging area is likely to be the reduction in innovation, which will harm all future generations of patients.

Although policymakers know that price controls can be very harmful, they continue to have strong incentives to legislate low prices for themselves. This often leads to the adoption of more sophisticated price controls. The government pegs its price to some reference price in the economy rather than choosing a fixed number, or sets its price a fixed amount below that of other customers. These schemes destroy welfare by inserting a new incentive into what would otherwise be a well-functioning market; either the price to non-government customers is higher or the price to poorer customers rises. More generally, the reference price chosen by the government rises because of the price control, not because of a change in the underlying forces of demand or supply.

The overwhelming evidence against price controls naturally leads to consideration of other methods of lowering purchasing costs. The private sector uses a number of methods that are both effective and consonant with a market economy. Such approaches, when used by the private market, are much less damaging to economic welfare than a government price control.

One disadvantage of the price system is that for certain products, the costs of setting up the industry are so high; there is only one seller of the product. In cases like these, such as with the electricity and the natural gas companies, or with the water companies, without government regulation, prices could be very expensive since they are the only providers of the product. In these cases, the government needs to regulate these industries because the price system would lead to very high prices for water, electricity, and natural gas. Since the setup costs for these industries are so high, there is no competition for these companies. This could cause consumers to make some very difficult choices if the prices are regulated by the government. In the price system, prices are used to determine what goods and services are produced and who gets them.

Conclusion

Summing up here and without forgetting what has been discussed above in this section, the government's practical regulatory price techniques are ceiling on prices and minimum prices. In an economy like that of Cameroon, the government resorts to price control in which all business establishments have to adopt the government's price policy[275] to control relative prices so as to achieve certain targets, to prevent inflationary price rise and to prevent abnormal increase in prices. All these and more are the various ways the government of Cameroon use to protect the costumer from exaggerated prices from producers and manufacturers of products and services. Where some producers, wholesalers and even retailers go against the pricing policy in Cameroon, they become liable.

[275] It should be recalled here that the government of Cameroon through the 2015 Law has categorised prices of products at different levels; Goods with homologated prices like zinc, cement, sugar etc. Goods whose prices are made or fixed after consultation between the Ministry in charge of prices and various sector operators. The last category of goods is those bought and sold under the free pricing mechanism.

5

OFFENCES AND SANCTIONS ON ILLEGAL AND UNLAWFUL PRICING OF PRODUCTS IN CAMEROON

Introduction

It should be said at the beginning here that any violation of the decrees, orders and decisions on prices issued pursuant to the law governing prices in Cameroon is considered as illegal and therefore forbidden. This especially is with regard to prices above the fixed retail price, prices below the minimum purchase or selling price of local products, maintained at the previous level, whereas they should have been reduced. This is evident in the recent squabbles between brewery companies and the Ministry of Trade in Cameroon over the increase in prices over alcoholic and non alcoholic drinks. It is also considered as unlawful price increase for any producer, industrialist or trader to keep products or commodities meant for sale by refusing to satisfy the buyers' requests on as available basis, so long as these requests do not show any anomaly, as well as habitually apply unjustified discriminatory price conditions through corresponding cost price increases.

It is also unlawful to restrict the sale or purchase of any product, raw material or commodity to some days, whereas the business undertakings or shops concerned are open for the sale of such products, raw materials or commodities, provided, however, that the sale of other articles is not subject to a special regulation. Also, to take or attempt to take an action, either individually or as a group or an association, aimed at circumventing price regulation by threatening to close down his or her commercial, industrial or craft activity, or by effectively closing down the activity is unlawful. Producers and manufacturers of goods and services sometimes refuse to present the required price justification documents to control officials, or present forged documents. Others go as far as selling above displayed, labeled or homologated prices.

Further, according to section 76 of the 2015 Law governing commercial activity in Cameroon, the following shall be considered as unlawful pricing and consequently forbidden;

- All product or service sale offers or proposals made or concluded at an unlawful price;
- All purchases or purchase offers intentionally made or concluded at an unlawful price;
- Maintaining the price of products or services whose quantity or weight has been reduced or the volume of whose container has been reduced;
- The paid intervention, in whatever form of an intermediary who occasionally or habitually gets involved, without being duly authorized in the distribution chain, leading to a rise in the lawful price of goods;
- The use of a false name to sell a low quality product at the price of a similar but higher quality product.

To add, the sale of an item of goods or provision of a service without prior submission of price or tariff lists or structures, for goods or services subject to that procedure is forbidden. Selling at prices unjustifiably imposed by the producer, industrialist, wholesaler or importer and also false cost price declarations intended to influence the prices of goods and services not subject to the free pricing system is as well forbidden.

It is equally forbidden for a trader to apply against another trader or compel same to apply discriminatory prices, payment deadlines and conditions of sale or purchase not justified by any valuable consideration that comply with fair and honest commercial practices.[276]

Sanctions for Illegal and Unlawful Pricing.

In Cameroon, there exist sanctions on illegal and unlawful pricing at two levels. There is the Administrative penalty on one hand and Criminal sanctions on the other.

[276] Section 78 of the 2015 Law governing commercial activity in Cameroon

Administrative sanctions

The Ministry of Trade in Cameroon has sworn civil servants or officials at the Regional, Divisional and Sub-divisional levels charged with the duty of price control. They have the competence to check prices of commodities in the various markets and on the shelves in stores. They control prices following the reference book[277] containing the various price units for the different categories of goods and services all over the national territory prepared at the Ministry of Trade and signed by the Minister. They have the capacity as laid down by the 2015 Law[278] to penalise traders, producers, wholesalers and retailers who do the not respect the price code, either by selling above the required price, refusal to communicate his or her price structure or scale and his/her general condition of sale to a reseller who so request; producer or retailer who does sales without prior or tariff homologation for goods and services whose prices or tariffs are subject to such a procedure, when these are noticed by the price controllers, they have the right to sanction such a trader or corporate body for violations of the law on prices.

The penalty at this level is the payment of fine of 10% of the annual turnover of the offending trader or professional with a minimum fine of 100.000 (one hundred thousand) francs CFA for a natural person and 250.000 (two hundred and fifty thousand) francs CFA for a legal person.[279] The violation of the provisions of this law by the offending trader or professional is equally punished with a fine of 5% of the annual turnover with a minimum price of 30.000 (thirty thousand) francs CFA for a natural person and 100.000 (one hundred thousand) francs CFA for a legal person.[280]

Criminal sanctions

As is the case with Administrative penalties observed above, the 2015 Law equally outlines some of the offences in commercial practices which are sanctioned by the Cameroon Penal Code on traders, corporate persons and producers of goods and services who do not respect the law on pricing. All corporate persons are responsible for the crimes or offences committed by their agents.[281] Where such offence was committed by both physical and

[277] As per the mercurial framework.
[278] *Ibid.*
[279] See section 91 (2).
[280] Section 91 (1).
[281] Section 74 of the Penal Code

moral persons either separately or one acting as an accomplice shall all be criminally liable.[282]

Anybody whoever incites to the obstruction of sworn administrative personnel from the Ministry of Trade who are carrying out a lawful[283] duty on price control shall be punished with imprisonment for from 3 (three) months to 4 (four) years.[284]This provision of the penal code is also supported by article 98 of the 2015 Law.[285]

According to section 256[286](1) and (2) of the Penal Code, who ever by any fraudulent means causes an artificial increase or decrease of the price of goods or public or private securities, shall be punished with imprisonment for from 2 (two) months to 2 (two) years and with fine of from CFA 400.000 (four hundred thousand) to CFA 20.000 000 (twenty million). The penalty shall be doubled where the goods in question are food stuffs or subjected to standard regulations.[287]

Furthermore, whoever so offers any goods to the public as to engender the hope of obtaining them free or of a reduced price in consideration of persuading others to take up coupons or to buy, or sends goods to an addressee who has not ordered them, giving him the choice between keeping them and sending them back whether or not at his expense shall be punished with imprisonment for from 1 (one) month to 1 (one) year or with fine of from CFA 200 000 (two hundred thousand) to CFA 2 000 000 (two million), or with both such imprisonment and fine.[288]

Conclusion

For any country to have a sustainable economic growth, it must have a good pricing policy as one of its back bones. Cameroon's level of commercial growth today reflects its pricing policy. Leaving the market in Cameroon to determine its pricing policy will be an erroneous event given that Cameron still has a good percentage of people who still live below a thousand francs per day, and if this happens, the poor will have a low purchasing power to buy

[282] See section 97 (1)(2)(3) of the 2015 Law on commercial activity in Cameroon on Penal Sanctions.
[283] See equally section 76 of the Penal Code.
[284] Section 157 of the Cameroon Penal Code.
[285] *Supra* .
[286] Rigging Prices.
[287] Section 98 (1) (c) of the 2015 Law.
[288] See section 98 (1) (e) of the 2015 Law (supra)

basic needs. It is for this reason that it is imperative for the government to step in and lay down policies that will help mitigate pricing. Prices of goods and services have been harmonized all over the national territory by the Ministry of Trade and to ensure this harmony, there are sworn administrative personnel from the same ministry who are charged with price control.

The pricing policy in Cameroon as enshrined in the 2015 Law governing commercial activities, and the provision of Price Reference Book (*Mecuriale de Reference*) which contains all the different price rubriques, indicates the government's "*Will*" to protect consumers and customers from unscrupulous different price rubriques, indicates the government's "*Will*" to protect consumers and costumers from unscrupulous business people from unnecessarily inflating or changing the prices of goods and services. Despite all these moves taken by the state, black market price still prevail in Cameroon. It is noticed that the pricing policy in Cameroon does not take into consideration the fact that increase in distance will normally lead to increase in price. For example, a bag of cement sold in Douala is cheaper than the same bag sold in Mora in the Far North Region of the country if supply were to come from Douala (in the Littoral Region). This and many other reasons explain why the pricing policy in Cameroon will hardly be absolute or a reality everywhere and all the time. There is therefore the urgent need for the government to effectively implement the laws in place in order to ensure a fair pricing system of goods in the marketplace. Such a measure will go a long way to establish a conducive business climate in fostering investment.

The experience of formal price laws suggests useful strategies for bringing other formal laws into the informal sector, although there are two principal ways in which formal price laws are not implemented effectively in Cameroon's informal sector. First, the authors' experience in the Cameroon markets show that formal business laws are neither enforced by the government nor respected by the traders. Second, the price control authorities are not taking the pro-price-morale steps of enhancing the likelihood of compliance; instead, the collection regime depends on a self-fueled money engine--a pyramid structure backed by coercion and bribery. Finally, even if formal price laws were applied consistently in the informal sector, the tax-morale strategies to enhance compliance translate with difficulty to the business arena because the role of government is much less direct in the business context.

6

REMEDIES FOR BREACH OF CONTRACT OF SALE OF GOODS BY THE SELLER

Introduction

This chapter is concerned with the duties of the seller under a contact of sale of goods. It specifically highlights the obligation of the seller to cure a non-conforming delivery of goods as governed by the OHADA Uniform Act on General Commercial Law, with emphasis on cases relating to defects of quality and discriminatory prices. The discussion here lies mostly on the remedies available to a commercial buyer because of the important business position he occupies between the seller and the consumer buyer. As a matter of fact and business efficacy, the commercial buyer is bound to accept delivery of the goods only when the seller may have delivered the goods in conformity with the contract stipulations. The question of 'cure' becomes a great concern to the commercial buyer in cases of the seller's act for non-delivery or for late delivery, or because the goods delivered fail to conform to the standard set by the express or implied terms of the contract. The difficulty here appears to link the buyer's rejection of the goods where payment of the goods may have been effected and the seller defaults in this duty to rightly deliver. This would represent a total failure of consideration by the seller and consequently, the buyer has a right of action on the contract. This paper has as objective to explore the consistent scheme set up by the Uniform Act in determining the seller's duty to cure a non-conforming delivery of goods before and after delivery, and the remedies that the buyer can resort to in the case of the seller's act of non-performance of such a duty.

In some legal systems, whether Common law or Civil law jurisdictions, upon conclusion of a contract of sale, parties are bound to perform their respective obligations. When a contracting party fails to perform or wrongly performs his obligations under the contract, the aggrieved party is thereupon entitled to seek relief. Generally, the purpose of granting relief upon breach of contract is to either enforce the natural purpose of the contract or to put the parties in the situation they would have been, if the contract was properly performed. Depending on the type of remedy sought, there are some remedies that may be exercised only unilaterally, some need to be granted by judicial decree while others are only granted out of court discretion.[289] Moreover, in particular circumstances, equitable remedies will also be awarded whenever adequate to ensure justice.

It must be noted that the harmonisation of business law in Africa is situated in this same line of reasoning. This is the case of the OHADA Uniform Act on General Commercial Law. It contains a comprehensive system of remedies for aggrieved buyers which pre-empts remedies available under domestic sales laws. Under the UAGCL, the remedy of specific performance is broad. In favour of the buyer, it can be exercised against the seller. In applying for specific performance, the buyer may require the seller to repair the goods,[290] or to substitute them,[291] or to withhold performance.[292]An additional period of time may also be granted for the seller to complete performance of his obligations.[293] Although the buyer has the right in certain circumstances of the breach to reduce the purchase price,[294] the seller's right to cure is meant to take over the former's right.

The purpose of this chapter therefore is to explore the consistent scheme set up by the Uniform Act in determining the seller's duty to cure a non-conforming delivery of goods and the remedies that the buyer can resort to in the case of the failure by the latter to perform his delivery obligations. The UAGCL treats separately and differently the seller's duty to cure a non-conforming delivery before and after delivery of the goods. The actual fact is to determine whether there is a fundamental breach as a result of the seller's non-performance of delivery to the buyer. Where the seller defaults in this duty, the buyer has a right of action on the contract. This would represent a total failure of consideration by the seller and consequently, the buyer has a right of action on the contract. This chapter shall not devote space to the seller's real remedies. It rather highlights the duty of a seller, either a paid or

289 Burrows, Andrew, *Torts and Breach of Contract*, 2nd edition, London, Butterworths, 1994, p. 1.
290 Article 283 paragraph (para.) 1 UAGCL.
291 Article 283 para.2 UAGCL.
292 Article 282 UAGCL.
293 Article 283 UAGCL.
294 Article 288 UAGCL.

an unpaid seller[295] who is directly entitled to receive the price.[296] Thus, such a distinction is not being made here as the focus of the discussion centres on the entire seller's ability and willingness to tender delivery[297] as prerequisites of his right to demand tender of the price.[298]

The Seller's Delivery Obligations

Unless otherwise agreed, delivery of the goods and payment of the price[299] are concurrent conditions. Under the UAGCL, the seller in a contract of sales has four main obligations including the obligation to deliver the goods, to handover any documents relating to them, to ensure that they are in conformity with the order and to provide guarantee over them.[300] Moreover, the seller is under the obligation to supply goods at the time agreed as stated in the contract of sale, otherwise, the default rule makes it clear that unless otherwise stated by the parties, time is not of essence in the contract of sale.[301] Also, the seller must provide to the buyer the guarantee that goods delivered are free from encumbrances and that he will enjoy quiet possession.[302]Hence, it is a fundamental obligation that the seller must fulfill his obligations as required by the contract. What Article 255 requires is not coincidence of performance of the delivery by the seller and payment obligations of the buyer but coincidence of willingness to perform. This is a clear application of the requirement of consideration inherent in the formation of a contract under Common law. The primary rule related to the place of delivery in both the UAGCL and the SGA is being determined by the parties in the contract.[303] It follows that if the contracting parties agree that the delivery be governed by the standard terms based on the Incoterms[304] shorthand description, the

[295] This is one who either has been paid in full, or who has accepted conditional payment by bill of exchange or other negotiable instrument or otherwise. See Bridge Michael, *The Sale of Goods*, New York, Oxford University Press Inc., 2003, p. 487.

[296] SGA s 38(1)

[297] Article 255 UAGCL.

[298] Article 262 UAGCL.

[299] Article 262 UAGCL.

[300] Article 255 UAGCL.

[301] Nigeria SGA 1893 s 10; as applicable in all northern and eastern States, for Lagos State SGA 1973, Western States SGA 1959 and Edo State SGA 1976.

[302] Article 260 UAGCL.

[303] Article 250–251 UAGCL.

[304] Incoterms or international commercial terms are a series of international sales terms, published by the International Chamber of Commerce (ICC) and widely used in international, regional and even domestic commercial transactions. They are also recognised globally by courts, governments, legal authorities and practitioners worldwide.

seller's delivery obligation will as a general rule be determined by the terms of their contract rather than the provision of the law.

Under the UAGCL, the default rules provides that, if the contract is silent on the place of delivery, the buyer is under the duty to take delivery where the goods were manufactured, or where they are stored, or at the place where the seller has his principal business.[305] Hence, the seller will make delivery available either at the place they are manufactured or where they are stored, or at the seller's main place of business.[306] Once they are made available, it is the buyer obligation to take delivery. In the Cameroonian case involving *Laborex c/ Mejo M'obam Moise,*[307] the TGI (High Court) of Mfoundi in Yaoundé held that in the absence of an agreement as to the place of delivery, the buyer who fails to take delivery at the seller's place of business cannot sue the seller for failing to perform his obligation to deliver.

Moreover, where the contract involves the transportation of goods, and the seller is not bound by any contractual term related to the place of delivery, the UAGCL provides that the seller will deliver the goods to the buyer as soon as they are handed over to the carrier.[308] Thus, it is clear that the goods will not be treated as delivered if the documents relating to the goods are handed over to the buyer instead of the goods. But rather it is important to note that the UAGCL purpose is to ensure the physical delivery of the goods to the carrier for the seller's obligation to be fulfilled.[309]When the delivery involves transportation of the goods, it may be inferred from the provision of the UAGCL that the moment of delivery is the moment the goods are handed over to the carrier for delivery to the buyer.[310]

The time of delivery is of the essence in the contract of sales. The seller must deliver the goods at the fixed date, if not a determinable date defined in the contract. If such a date is not provided, the delivery will rather be made in the fixed period of time, fixed or determinable from the contract.[311] If the parties totally fail to determine the moment for delivery, it will automatically be considered to take place within a reasonable time from the time the contract is concluded.[312] Generally, what amounts to reasonable time is left to

---

305 Article 251 (b) UAGCL.

306 *Ibid.*

307 TGI Mfoundi, n° 246, 4–3–2002: *MejoM'ObamMoïse c/ Stéanonyme LABOREX Cameroun*, available at www.ohada.com, Ohadata J-04–216.

308 Article 252 para. 1 UAGCL.

309 *Ibid*

310 Article252 para. 1 UAGCL.

311 Article 253 para. 1–2UAGCL.

312 Article 253 para. 3UAGCL.

the court to decide in light with the will of the contracting parties.[313] Also, it is argued that the court might take into account usage[314] or the nature of the goods. For instance, the reasonable period of perishable goods will require a lesser time of delivery than if the contract of sales was about an engine to be delivered.[315]

The question of Instalmental delivery[316] seems not to be clearly highlighted under the new UAGCL, where the seller is given an opportunity to remedy the non-conforming part(s) of goods before delivery. As a justification for this, it could be advanced that the Uniform Act tends to avoid a multiplicity of contracts by imposing on the seller the duty to make a single tender of goods covering the entirety of the goods. However, from a cursory reading of the provisions of UAGCL this kind of delivery is not imposed by law but left to the parties to decide. The conjunction of Article 255 and 289 UAGCL prompts the question whether the seller may call upon the buyer to accept any instalment at all if it is plain that the seller will be unable to deliver the whole of the contractually agreed amount of the goods or just the missing part(s). By the wordings of Article 289, it may be implied that matters of quantitative lapses and time by the seller are more dealt with. Consequently, if the buyer rejects the non-conforming part of a tender while accepting the rest, he is not obliged to accept a fresh tender. The buyer is rather entitled to damages and interests relating to the non-conforming delivery of the goods.

The Seller's Duty to Cure a Non-Conforming Delivery Prior to the Buyer's Acceptance of the Goods

In the first place, the Uniform Act gives the seller an unfettered right to cure any non-conformity prior to the date set for delivery by the contract.[317] It is a right because the time for the seller's performance has not yet expired within the agreed contract time with the buyer. This therefore gives him the right to make a conforming delivery before the lapse of the performance. However, it remains a duty on the part of the seller to deliver the conforming goods to the buyer for acceptance in accordance with the terms of the

313 Article 238 para. 1–2 UAGCL; Akuété Pedros Santos & Jean YadoToé, *OHADA Droit Commercial Général,* Bruxelles, Bruylant, Collection Droit Uniforme Africain, 2002,p. 391.

314 Art icle 239 para. 1–2 UAGCL.

315 Akuété Pedros Santos & Jean YadoToé, *OHADA Droit Commercial Général, Op. cit.,*p. 391.

316 An instalment contract is defined as one "which requires or authorises the delivery of goods in separate lots to be separately accepted . . ." See the American Uniform Commercial Code-U.C.C. § 2–612 (1); Article 73 CISG; Sale of Goods Act, 1979, s 31.

317 Article 257 UAGCL.

contract. These rights of the seller include delivery of a part or a missing quantity or new goods in replacement of goods that do not conform to the contract, or to cure any defect of goods which do not conform to the contract. The seller's right to cure before the date of performance depends on whether he reasonably believed that a non-conforming tender was acceptable to the commercial buyer. By way of explanation, the Uniform Act does not explain the circumstances which may lead the seller to cure in anticipation delivery of the goods to the buyer. By inference, the language of the Uniform Act allows one to believe that the seller's right to cure before the delivery date may arise only if he actually knew of the non-conformity of tender at the time of performance. The question is to know what may push the seller to remedy any defect before delivery of the goods to the buyer.

However, the Uniform Act has suggested some instances that the seller may find it necessary to cure. This may be as a result of a non-delivery of a missing part or a missing quantity or new goods in replacement of goods that do not conform to the contract, or to remedy any defect of conformity.[318] The choice is left to the seller as long as cure is possible by any means within a reasonable time. Therefore, it must be clear that the seller's non-performance of delivery of conforming goods within this context is considered to be a non-fundamental breach of contract because basically the seller has the opportunity to cure the situation to afford satisfaction to the buyer. The purpose of the law here is geared at preserving the contractual bond between the parties under their contract of sale. In this view, 'cure' may be effected on two situations. Firstly, a commercial buyer faced with defective goods may elect not to reject them but to allow the seller to replace or repair them before the expiration of the time set for delivery. The form which 'cure' would take would vary according to whether the contract was for unascertained or specific goods. Under a contract for unascertained goods the seller could 'cure' by delivering replacement goods matching the contract description. Under a contract for specific goods, the seller could only 'cure' by repairing the goods.[319]

Secondly, another thought could be that a seller should be found to have had reasonable cause to believe that his tender would have been rejected by the buyer because he had some reason such as prior course of dealing or trade usage which reasonably led him to believe that the goods would not be accepted.At this point in time, the seller has full knowledge of the facts before

[318] Article 257 UAGCL; Leisinger, K. Benjamin, *Fundamental Breach- Considering Non-Conformity of the Goods*, Germany, European Law Publishers GmbH, 2007, p.62.

[319] Malaurie, Philippe et al, *Droit Civil, Les Contrats Spéciaux*, 3e édition, Montchrestien, L.G.D.J., pp.182–183.

the goods in question reach the buyer. This is salutary as the seller is expected to be of good faith and show a great sense of prudent business behaviour.

A final approach, which is arguable, is that the Uniform Act should neither nor only pays attention to the fact that '...the exercise of such right causes damage or expenses to the buyer'.[320] This is rather insufficient as the courts should rather pay attention to the severity of the breach even though at this point, it does not cause any harm to the buyer. The idea that the greater the non-conformity, the less reasonable the seller's belief that the goods will be acceptable, seems reasonable, but is not literally stated in the Uniform Act. In other words, the Uniform Act is silent on the fundamentality of the seller's breach as compared to other legal systems.[321]The Uniform Act has not expressly stated that non-conformity must be minor or severe for the seller to have a right to cure. Thus, is the seller allowed to cure only mostly minor non-conformities, in other to satisfy the buyer's reasonable expectations? It is, however, regrettable that the new Uniform Act as compared to the former, does not define or distinguish between the issues of "fundamental breach" or what comprises substantial non-conformity.[322]

However, it is also relevant to note that upon the seller's breach due to failure to deliver, avoidance of the contract can only be made possible through a petition by the buyer to the competent court, depending on the nature and gravity of the breach.[323] Avoidance of the contract due to failure to deliver is therefore judicial under the Uniform Act as opposed to the unilateral avoidance under the United Nations Convention on the International Sale of Goods (CISG).[324] As a matter of fact, it is expressly clear that OHADA is for the judicial process of cancellation of the contract,[325] as well as the anticipated action for avoidance when before the date of the performance of the contract, it appears that one party will not fulfill an essential part of his obligation due to some circumstances beyond his control.[326] The buyer may apply to the court for cancellation of the contract if the seller's breach of the contract is

[320] Article 257UAGCL.

[321] Article 25 CISG; Article 7.3.1 UNIDROIT Principles of International Commercial Contracts, 2004.

[322] This was the position under Article 246- 248 of the old Uniform Act; Under the former UAGCL, fundamental breach is known in as "essential breach" or in French as *manquement essential;* Nsie, E., "La Sanction de l'Inexécution de la Vente Commerciale en Droit Uniforme Africain", (2003) *Revue Afrique et Politique,* Vol. 2, no 1, p. 3.

[323] Article 281 UAGCL.

[324] Martor, Boris et al, *Business Law in Africa, OHADA and the Harmonization Process,* London, GMB Publishing Ltd., 2nd edition, 2002,p. 64; Pougoué, Paul-Gérard & Kalieu Elongo, Yvette Rachel *Introduction Critique a l'OHADA,* Yaoundé, P.U.A., 2008, p.153.

[325] Article 281 UAGCL.

[326] Article 282 UAGCL.

a serious one provided the buyer had notified the seller of his decision. The buyer nevertheless retains all other remedies, such as the right to claim damages or a reduction in price. Arguably, this position of the Uniform Act revolves around the issue of the fundamentality of the seller's breach to be raised by the buyer. The consequence is that the buyer has the right to avoid the contract if he can establish to the courts the existence of the seller's fundamental breach of contract. Thus, the issue of fundamentality of breach is left for the judge to interpret.The burden of proof lies on the buyer. One reason for incorporating such onerous standards into the Uniform Act is to protect the seller.

In Common Law jurisdictions, fundamental breach refers to a breach which goes to "the root of the contract"[327]or which results in performance "totally different from that which the contract contemplates" with the effect of depriving the aggrieved party from achieving the main purpose for which he contracted for and entitle the aggrieved party to sue for damages.[328] In this sense, the breach shall be related to a fundamental term, a breach of condition or a breach of warranty which constitutes the reason of the aggrieved party (buyer) to put an end to the contract. However, as to the question of what term or condition amounts to a fundamental breach, it is a question of construction depending on every particular case.

The emphasis in the above instances is less on the seller's knowledge of the defect or reasonable belief in the acceptability of the non-conforming tender than on the basis of the parties' agreement. It is of prime importance that the buyer should receive what he bargained for rather than on the seller's belief of the likelihood of the acceptability of the goods by the buyer when delivered. In other words, the duty of right delivery[329] by the seller favours the parties' expectations under the contract rather than the seller's reasonable belief that the goods will be accepted. The right of the seller to cure a defective tender by making a fresh tender of conforming goods before delivery is in accord with commercial practice. The seller is as a rule entitled to do this if he still has time under the contract which conforms with the contract, in which event,

[327] *Suisse Atlantique Sociétéd'Armement Maritime S.A v. N.V. Rotterdamsche Kolen Centrale* [1967] 1 A.C. 361 p 399 [1966] 1 Lloyd's Rep. 529 p 545 (H.L); It was latter reaffirmed on appeal by Lord Denning in the House of Lords decision in *Photo Productions Ltd. v. Securicor Transport Ltd.* It was held that a fundamental breach in a contract is a breach of a fundamental term, that is, a breach of condition that "goes to the root of the contract". Also, the two cases reaffirmed that fundamental breach is strictly a question of construction of the contract. In all, a fundamental breach is therefore found only through examining the reasonable intentions of the parties at the time of entering into contract.

[328] J. Ademola Yakubu, *Law of Contract in Nigeria*, Mathouse Press Limited, 2003, p. 259.

[329] Article 255 para. 1 UAGCL.

the buyer is bound to accept the goods so tendered. Consequently, the buyer's remedies on account of the seller's non-fundamental breach of contract are the rights to require repair or replace the goods.At Common law, this is well illustrated by the decision of the Court of Appeal in *Borrowman Phillips & Co v Free & Hollis.*[330]The sole rejection of the goods by the buyer is to nullify delivery in case the seller does not perform this right.

The Seller's Duty to Cure a Non-Conforming Delivery after the Date of Performance

The seller's right to cure after the date of performance, depends on whether a non-conforming delivery was acceptable by the buyer. By Article 258 of the Uniform Act, the seller is allowed to cure after the delivery date only if he actually knew of the non-conformity of tender of goods at the time of performance brought to his knowledge by the buyer. The buyer has a period of one year to lay his action from the moment he discovers any defects in the non-conforming delivery of the goods. In actual fact, the buyer must report to the seller any defects which he may have happened to discover after accepting delivery of the goods. The perishability of the goods, cost of repairs by the seller and time for waiting by the buyer are some important factors to be considered which may impair the buyer's business. Though the express language of Article 259 of the Uniform Act does not indicate the possibility for the seller to cure, cure is not excluded by Article 257. Perhaps the most troubling question is whether the seller may cure a material breach in a situation where the buyer accepts the goods, by holding them beyond the time necessary for inspection, and then gives notice that he is revoking that acceptance. As a justification for this, the law should apply a policy of minimization of economic waste which strongly supports recognition of a reasonable opportunity for cure.

It is less difficult to predict when a seller has a right to cure a late or non-conforming performance under the Uniform Act. Even though the buyer's rejection or revocation is timely within a one year period giving the seller the possibility to cure during that time-frame, the Uniform Act is rather silent on the time-frame for the seller to cure after the buyer's revocation of acceptance. In this situation, the seller should strive to minimize economic loss on the side of the buyer. A re-tender is not necessarily too late because the contract date for delivery has passed. By reasoning, the rules as to time

330 (1878) 4 QBD 500.

for a re-tender are the same as those for the original tender as stipulated in the contract.[331] For the sake of a good trading relationship, time is of essence here in doing business for the commercial buyer, especially in a large -scale commodity dealings with consumer buyers.[332] On this view, the agreement to replace or repair the defective goods is not a rescission or variation of the original contract of sale but simply an action to execute a fresh act of performance. However, it would all depend on the circumstances and on the mutual agreement of the parties. It is worthy of note that, the Uniform Act has allowed buyers to reject or revoke acceptance, despite the seller's willingness to repair, in situations in which it is plausible that the cost of the seller's investment outweighs the benefits conferred upon the buyer.[333] By analogy, the law would not allow the buyer to refuse cure where the cost of cure to the seller and the cost to the buyer of waiting are low or when the buyer's refusal to allow cure was motivated by a change in the market price or his information about the goods. Resources are scarce relative to society's needs and, hence, waste of such resources should be prevented.[334]

From an economic standpoint, the efficient resolution between the buyer's and the seller's rights following a non-conforming delivery by the seller is one that "minimizes the joint allocative costs of the transaction."[335] To determine the joint allocative cost, the cost to the seller to cure a defective delivery, say eight hundred thousands CFA F, is added to the buyer's cost for loss of use and any consequential damages, say two hundred thousands CFA F. The combined cost, one million CFA F, is then compared to the seller's cost of re-disposing of the goods. If the cost to the seller of reselling the goods is more than the cost of allowing the seller to cure, the seller will be permitted to cure the tender. In an international transaction, the cost of resale is magnified since the seller is dealing in a foreign market. Arguably, the same efficiency could be achieved by allowing the buyer to negotiate with the seller for damages to an amount equalling one million CFA F.

The seller's duty to cure under the Uniform Act is qualified by certain rights and duties allowed the buyer. If the law allows the buyer to make known whether he will accept delivery of the goods by reporting any defects

---

331 Goode, Roy, *Commercial Law,* 3rd edition, Penguin Books, 2004, pp. 334.

332 Bradgate, Robert, *Commercial Law,* 3rd edition, Oxford University Press, 2005, p.312.

333 Article 257 UAGCL; Akuété Pedros Santos & Jean YadoToé, *OHADA Droit Commercial Général, Op. cit.,* p. 392.

334 Leisinger, K. Benjamin, *Fundamental Breach- Considering Non-Conformity of the Goods, Op. cit.,* p. 26.

335 Priest, Breach and Remedy for the Tender of Non conforming Goods under the Uniform Commercial Code: An Economic Approach, (1978) 91 *Harvard Law Review* 960.

in the goods to the seller for cure, the seller may perform as from the time of his request in order to cure the problem. By implication, the buyer may not, during that period of time, resort to any remedy which is inconsistent with performance by the seller. But this could be the reverse in case the seller fails to perform this right, allowing the buyer the opportunity to use other adequate remedies for the seller's non-conforming of performance.

Remedies available to the Buyer in the event of Non-Conforming Delivery

Specific Peformance

Under the UAGCL, the remedy of specific performance is considered as the "natural" or primary remedy upon breach of contract.[336] The purpose for a contracting party to compel performance of the contract is nothing but to ensure the proper execution of the contract despite the breach.[337] In other words, the reason of the claim is to place the aggrieved party in the position he would have been if the obligation from the other party was fully performed.

Whether the breach of contract occurs as a result of the non-performance or bad performance, the UAGCL provides for the remedy of specific performance which can be exercised by a contracting party to enforce the natural performance of the contract be it the complete or partial fulfilment of his obligations.[338]Basically, when the breach of seller's obligation to deliver conforming goods under the Uniform Act amounts to a breach, (but not regarded as fundamental) instead for the buyer to petition for the avoidance of the contract, he may still use the option, for instance in case of non-conformity of the goods, to require specific performance from the seller to supply substituted goods.[339] But when the breach is less severe, that is, does not constitute a fundamental breach, then the specific performance may require the seller either to repair the goods,[340] withhold performance[341] or an additional time may be granted for the seller to complete performance of his

[336] Akuété Pedros Santos & Jean Yado Toé, *OHADA Droit Commercial Général, Op. cit.*,p. 420.
[337] Harris, Donald & Denis, *Contract Law Today Anglo-French Comparisons,* Oxford, Clarendon Press, 1989, p. 249.
[338] Article 281–282 UAGCL.
[339] Article 283 para.1 UAGCL.
[340] Article 283 para.2 -284 UAGCL.
[341] Article 282 UAGCL.

obligation.[342] In this situation, the buyer is generally considered to have two alternatives: to adopt the contract or to reject the goods and thereby treat the contract as discharged, based on the gravity of the breach.[343] As a question of time and commercial urgency, a typical buyer will inform the seller that the goods are not conforming to the contract stipulations and requests that they be repaired or replaced. It could conveniently be understood here that the attitude of the Uniform Act in this line of reasoning is to maintain a contractual bond between the seller and the buyer by holding the contract open for performance by allowing a fresh tender by the seller.[344]

There are instances at Common Law where the remedy of damages turns inadequate in favour of a decree of specific performance. Specific performance at Common Law is an equitable remedy. It is issued at the discretion of Common Law court, particularly when the Common law remedy has been found inadequate or with inappropriate relief.[345] In fact, as per JSC in *Universal Vulcanizing (Nig.) Ltd. v. I.U.T.T.C.*[346] specific performance is aimed at constraining a contracting party to do that which he has promised to do. Moreover, it is a remedy for breach of contract provided by equity to meet those cases where the Common law remedy of damages is inadequate.[347]

The Buyer's Duty to Give Notice of Non-conforming Tender

The UAGCL provides two instances where the buyer should give notice to the seller for any lack of conformity over the goods being delivered: the buyer must give notice of a lack of conformity discovered a month later from the day of delivery.[348] Failure to observe these requirements, the buyer will be

---

342 Article 283 para.2 UAGCL.

343 Article 281 para. 2 UAGCL.

344 Nguebou, Josette, *Le Droit Commercial Général dans l'Acte Uniforme OHADA,* Collection Droit Uniforme OHADA, Yaoundé, P.U.A., p.76 ; Jean Claude James, "La Vente Commerciale OHADA, Précurseur d'un Droit Harmonisé des Contrats?", Actes du Colloque International de Libreville sur *"Les Pratiques Contractuelles d'Affaires et les Processus d'Harmonisation dans les Espaces Régionaux"*, Octobre 26–28, 2011, pp.26–48, p.42–44.

345 G.H. Treitel, The *Law of Contract*, 10th edition, London, Sweet & Maxwell, 1999,p. 22.

346 [1962] NWLR 73. Similar statements were also made in *Afrotech v. MIA [2001] 6 WRN 65.*

347 Furmston,, Michael, *Cheshire, Fifoot and Furmston's Law of Contract*, 12th edition, Butterworths, p. 797.As it is the case in most common law jurisdictions, it is also a settled law in majority of the courts in Africa of Common Law tradition that on a claim for specific performance, courts have the power to award damages either in addition to or in lieu of the specific performance. It is immaterial in this case whether damages have specifically been claimed or not. *Ibedewelu v. Lawal [1971] 1All NLR; Universal Vulcanizing (Nig.) Ltd. v. I.U.T.T.C [1962] NWLR 73.*

348 Article 257 UAGCL.

deprived of his right to claim redress of the non-conformity. Secondly, the buyer must give notice of a hidden defect of conformity within one year from the moment when this was revealed or ought to be known.[349] To this effect, notice is therefore necessary in order to give the seller the opportunity to cure any deficiency in exercise of his duty of conformity. It also gives adequate right to the buyer to claim other remedies.[350]

The seller is entitled to treat the notice of the buyer of lack of conformity as binding on the buyer, who cannot himself be heard to deny the effectiveness of his own notice. The buyer may lose his right to reject the non-conforming goods by conduct which is inconsistent with rejection before, at the time of or subsequent to his notice. So by the buyer's conduct, his notice is ineffective if at the time of giving the notice he proceeds to sell the goods or does some other act which is inconsistent with rejection, for he cannot complain and improperly do another thing. As a rule, rejection of the goods by notice reverts title in the goods to the seller. Consequently, the seller is entitled to recover the goods in order to cure the defects within a reasonable time. In determining what is reasonable, it is necessary in this case to consider the interests of the buyer as well as those of the seller. Both parties are professional businessmen and time is of prime importance to both.

At this juncture, it is the duty of the buyer to hold the goods available for collection by the seller at the contractual place for examination.[351]However, it may happen that the non-conforming goods are perishable or fragile and may deteriorate by the time they get back to the seller as a result of the buyer's notice of lack of conformity. As a solution to this, the Uniform Act instructs the buyer to take reasonable steps to ensure the safety of the goods, by storing them in the warehouse of a third party at the expense of the seller, provided the costs are not unreasonable.[352]

There is no requirement as to a specific form of notice under the Uniform Act. Notice need not be written.[353]It may be given, by word of mouth, for example by telephone. However, as a matter of evidence, pursuant to Article 240 UAGCL, the buyer can simply prove it by using all possible means.

---

[349] Article259 UAGCL; Under the CISG, the time frame is 2 years, Article 39 CISG; Jérôme Huet, *Contrats Civils et Commerciaux, Responsabilité du Vendeur et Garantie Contre les Vice Cachés,* Paris, Litec, 1987, p.42.

[350] Articles 282, 283 and 284 UAGCL.

[351] Article 251 UAGCL.

[352] Article 272–274 UAGCL.

[353] The word 'written' shall mean any communication using a written medium, including the telegram, telex, telefax or e-mail; Ghestin, Jacques, *Conformité et Garanties dans la Vente (produits mobiliers),* Paris, LGDJ, 1983, p.212.

The Buyer's Ability to Require Delivery of Substitute or Repair of Goods

If the goods do not conform to the contract, the buyer as an alternative to avoidance may require delivery of substitute goods.[354] The buyer may require repair of the goods by the seller, unless this is unreasonable having regards to all circumstances.[355]If this is possible, the buyer may require the seller to remedy the lack of conformity by repair and fix an additional period of time for this purpose.[356] If the goods perish before the defect is repaired, the buyer may resort to other remedies with respect to the seller's breach of contract because repair is no longer workable. This solution follows from Article 283 paragraph 2 and 3 of the Uniform Act, which applies where the buyer has fixed "additional period of time for performance by the seller of his obligations" and may be expanded, by analogy, to cases in which such period has not been fixed. A different solution would encourage the buyer to avoid the contract by allowing for the repair of the goods.[357]

It follows therefore from the above discussion that three conditions must be satisfied for the buyer to exercise his right upon the seller's breach. There must be non-conformity of the goods according to the contractual provisions. The breach of conformity must be a fundamental breach (that is, for full avoidance by the buyer) and finally, the request to substitute the goods must be within a reasonable time frame allocated for such a breach and be complied with. In the second case, upon the seller's breach due to non-conformity of the goods at delivery, the buyer may request the seller to remedy the non-conformity by repair.[358] In his claim, the buyer must comply with the requirements of notice and the time-frame.[359]

Also, the law has provided for the seller, an opportunity to cure his breach, that is, replacement of the goods or repair of non-conforming goods) before[360] and after the date of delivery provided the buyer agrees.[361] This opportunity is often called self-execution. For instance, if the breach is about the delivery

[354] Articles 258, 259, 283 para. 2 UAGCL.

[355] Article 257 UAGCL; Huet, Jérôme, *Contrats Civils et Commerciaux, Responsabilité du Vendeur et Garantie Contre les Vice Cachés, Op. cit.*, p.430.

[356] Malaurie, Philippe et al, *Droit Civil, Les Contrats Spéciaux, Op. cit.*, p.203.

[357] Bollée, Sylvain, "Theory of Risks in the 1990 Vienna Sale of Goods Convention", (1999–2000) available on *Pace Institute of International Commercial Law, at http:/www.cisgw3.law.pace.edu*, pp.245–290,p.33.

[358] Article 257 UAGCL.

[359] Article 258 UAGCL.

[360] Articles 257 & 290 para.1UAGCL ; Mba-Owono, Charles, "Non-conformité et vices cachés dans la vente commerciale en droit uniforme africain", (2000) 41 *Juridis Périodique*, pp. 107–127, p. 122.

[361] Article 283 para.2 UAGCL.

of the missing part or quantity of the goods or substitution of the goods, in case of an anticipated delivery, the seller's willingness to remedy the breach amounts to a self-execution.[362] In other words, the seller needs not be given notice for remedy, provided the remedy takes place before the fixed date for delivery. However, the attempt to remedy may give rise to damages if it causes to the buyer unreasonable inconvenience or additional costs.[363]

The availability of such a choice of the performance-oriented buyers' remedy suggests that the Uniform Act favours remedies that preserve the contractual bond in contrast to remedies that involve termination of the contract, (that is, avoidance).

The issue of failed repair should also be considered here. Accordingly, if the buyer wants to rely on an unsuccessful repair by the seller in an attempt to deliver the missing part(s) of the goods as stipulated in Article 283 para. 2 and 3 of the Uniform Act, he must give notice of the fact that the lack of conformity failed, and this is irrespective of any notice already given before delivery of the repaired goods. Even though the seller may remedy the breach at his own expense, the buyer can, however, oppose this or claim for damages ensuing from the delayed performance.[364]

The issue of the seller's act to repair or substitute goods may seem doubtful on the part of the buyer with respect to the character or quality of the goods. A buyer might naturally be sceptical of repair work that the seller is forced to do under an order of a court or arbitral tribunal. This or the alternative of avoiding the contract and purchasing substitute goods eliminates doubts about the quality of repair work performed by the seller that has delivered non-conforming goods.[365] Of course, if the seller has repair capabilities not possessed by others, and the buyer cannot easily avoid the contract and replaces the goods, forcing the seller to repair pursuant to Articles 257 and 283 para.1 and 2 of the Uniform Act may be the buyer's only practical course, but such cases, apparently are rare. In addition, the buyer might well be concerned with the delay of waiting for a court or arbitral tribunal to order the seller to repair.[366]

[362] Ingeborg Schwenzer, "Buyer's Remedies in the case of Non-Conforming: Some Problems in a core area of the CISG", (2007)101 *Am. Soc'y Int'll Proc.* 416,p. 606; Akuété Pedro Santos & Jean Yado Toé, *OHADA Droit Commercial Général, Op. cit.*, p. 422.

[363] Gomez, Jean René, "Un Nouveau Droit de la Vente Commerciale en Afrique", (1999) *Revue Penant*, pp.145–185, p.175.

[364] Article 284 UAGCL.

[365] Goode, Roy, Commercial Law, *Op. cit.*, p.344.

[366] Flechner, Harry M., "Buyers' Remedies in General and Buyers' Performance-Oriented Remedies", (2005–2006) 25 (339) *Journal of Law and Commerce*, pp. 339–347, p. 343, (available online at www.heinonline.org).

Furthermore, it is, however, regrettable to understand some difficulties which may be related to the seller's duty to make a fresh tender of goods in conformity to the contractual terms, in view to remedy his breach of lack of conformity. Is the buyer bound to accept the goods tendered? In fact, it is hard to justify an obligation for the seller of selecting different goods to be delivered or to perform a second delivery with conforming goods. That would mean to substitute the performance of an obligation which does not exist. Where would such an obligation come from? A buyer's right to demand substitute goods is potentially expensive to a seller since substitution means retrieval or re-disposing of the goods first delivered.[367] Often in the case of raw materials or fungible goods, a breach is neither fundamental (it does not give rise to a right to demand substitute goods) nor repairable. In this situation, a buyer must keep the goods and take a reduction in price or sue for damages.

In addition, how many times should the seller correct his improper delivery to bring the result up to the expectations of the buyer? How long would it take for professional traders to include in their written general conditions an exemption from such an obligation in order to safe time in business dealings?[368] As a matter of fact, time is of essence here on the part of the commercial buyer in his business. It is, however, regrettable that opportunity has not been taken to revisit the OHADA Uniform Act by including express provisions as to this right of re-tender, a right which mitigates the impact of an improperly motivated rejection by the buyer, while at the same time tending to avoid economic waste.[369]

Obviously, according to the OHADA Law, the buyer is not quite deprived of all protection. He may avail himself of the guarantee provided by a default rule that grants him the right of complaining of the defects existing at the moment of the conclusion of the contract,[370] or from the time of delivery[371] within a short term of time and to start an action in court within the time

[367] Schneider, Eric C., "The Seller's Right to Cure under the Uniform Commercial Code and the United Nations Convention Code on Contract for the International Sale of Goods", (1989) 7 Arizona Journal of International and Comparative Law, pp. 1–27,p.4.

[368] Ferreri, Silva, "Remarks Concerning the Implementation of the CISG by the Courts. (The Seller's Performance and Article 35)", (2005–2006) 25, Journal of Law and Commerce, pp.224–225, p.224, available online at www.heinonline.org.

[369] The right to re-tender given by s 2 -508 of the Uniform Commercial Code (UCC) could be useful here.

[370] Article 1477 of the Italian Civil Code also strengthens this point in ordering the seller to "... deliver the good(s) in the condition which it was at the moment of the sale."

[371] Article 256 UAGCL.

limit of one year from the delivery.[372]

Avoidance of Contract in case of Tender of Non-conforming Goods

Under the UAGCL, if the seller tenders goods not conforming to the contract- for example, because they do not correspond with the contract stipulations or are unfit for the known purpose, the buyer may: (i) reject the goods and, if the seller is not able or willing to re-tender substitute goods in due time, treat the contract as repudiated, and sue for damages for non-delivery.[373]

The effect of the of the buyer's lawful rejection of the goods is to render the situation as if delivery had not been performed. It is worth stating that since there is a contractual duty on the part of the seller not to deliver non-conforming goods,[374] the buyer on avoiding the contract, can, (it is implied), include as part of his claim any expenses rendered futile in connection with the re-delivery.[375] For example, the costs incurred in taking possession of the goods and installing them prior to rejection.[376] This applies even though the risk has passed and the goods have been lost or damaged. Thus, the effect of the remedy of avoidance is to throw back the risk upon the seller.[377] The seller who collects or delays in collecting the goods after notice of rejection is liable for damages for storage costs in a warehouse for example, incurred by the buyer.[378]

The basis on which damages may be considered in the event of lack of conformity is whether the goods are bought for use or resale. A first element which should be taken into account is measuring the possibility for the commercial buyer to still make use of the goods or resell them. No fundamental breach is to be found when the buyer can still satisfactorily resell the goods in a normal business environment without incurring any inconveniences.[379] Because of the commercial necessity to resell the goods,

---

[372] Article 259 para.1 and 2 UAGCL.

[373] Article 283 para. 2 UAGCL; Philippe Malaurie *et al.*, *Droit Civil, Les Contrats Spéciaux, Op. cit.*, p. 204.

[374] Article 255 UAGCL.

[375] Article 283 para. 2 UAGCL.

[376] Goode, Roy, *Commercial Law, Op. cit.*, p. 377.

[377] Bollée, Slyvain, "Theory of Risks in the 1990 Vienna Sale of Goods Convention", *Op. cit.*, p. 57; Erauw, Johan, "CISG Articles 66–70: The Risk of Loss and Passing It", (2005) 25 *Journal of Law and Commerce*, pp. 1–13, p. 11.

[378] Article 272–274 UAGCL.

[379] Leisinger, K. Benjamin, *Fundamental Breach- Considering Non-Conformity of the Goods*, Germany, European Law Publishers GmbH, 2007, pp. 55–56.

the fact that the buyer might be forced in this situation to do so at a lower price is not to be regarded in itself, as an unreasonable hardship. Likewise, the unreasonable difficulty may also stem from the fact that the goods were produced in a country different from the one agreed upon in the contract, and subjected at the time to an international embargo. The buyer in this case has to prove unreasonable difficulties in trading the goods in his own country.[380] Apart from the possibility of reselling the goods, the buyer can still seek to be reimbursed for loss of income-profit and for any expenditure incurred in taking reasonable steps in either procuring the temporary use of comparable goods or the loss of deprivation of the use of the asset or the period of the delay in view to mitigate the loss.[381]

In another respect, the rejection may also relate to the part of the non-conforming goods. Article 289 of the Uniform Act allows for partial avoidance of the contract for non-delivery or non-conformity of only a part of the goods. In fact, the buyer who accepted part of the goods is precluded from rejecting the rest, for he is not obliged to accept delivery by instalments.[382] The buyer is expected to accept part while only entitled to claim for damages relating to the non-conformity part(s) of the goods. In some cases, the buyer cannot be compelled to accept a fresh delivery as to the part rejected, for he is not obliged to accept delivery by instalments under the Uniform Act.[383]The principle of severability is at work here in Article 289 UAGCL in laying down a separate rule for terminating instalmental contracts. The existence of severable rejection rights is implicit in Article 289 which permits the buyer to accept only part of a non-conforming instalment and reject the rest while the entire contract remains intact. In other words, the repudiation of the contract affects only the outstanding balance of the seller's performance and therefore, does not give the buyer the right to treat the whole contract as repudiated. It is clear that if the seller refuses to re-deliver the missing part(s) or non-conforming part(s), he commits a breach which the buyer is entitled to treat as discharging the entire contract. Normally, this will depend on the buyer's request.

However, because of some commercial necessity, the commercial buyer under the Uniform Act may decide to accept a fresh delivery of the

380 Veneziano, Anna, "Non-Conformity of Goods in International Sales; A Survey of Current Case law on CISG" (1997) 1 *International Business Law Journal*, pp.39–62, p.57.

381 Goode, Roy, *Commercial Law*, *Op. cit.*, p. 376.

382 Sale of Goods Act, 1979, s 31.

383 Article 247 of the former Uniform Act on General Commercial Law offered the opportunity for delivery by instalments; Akuété Pedro Santos & Jean Yado Toé, *OHADA Droit Commercial Général*, *Op. cit.*, p. 412.

non-conforming part of the goods if the seller is still within the contract period.[384] The reason for this is that in every contract there is an implied condition that the party undertaking an obligation shall continue to be willing and able to perform up to the date of performance. If, therefore, the seller's contract evinces either an intention to repudiate or an inability to perform,[385] the buyer is entitled to treat the contract as repudiated by what is usually termed anticipatory breach. But the delivery of something entirely different from what had been agreed might be considered as "non-delivery" and that it may give way to an immediate right for the buyer to avoid the contract.[386]The UAGCL does not differentiate between the delivery of an *aliudpro alio* (delivery of the wrong goods) and the delivery of a *peius* (delivery of non-conforming goods). Whether the delivery of an *aliud* or the delivery of a *peius,* they both fall within the unique concept of "non-conformity" and therefore, subject to the same remedies.[387]In furtherance to this, it is a total deviation of the seller's obligation to perform according to the contract stipulations.

Avoidance of the Contract in case of Non-conforming Documents

What rather constitutes "documents" in the UAGCL has not been defined.[388] But the seller's duty to deliver under the Uniform Act is thus not a distinct and isolated obligation but encompasses all the seller's obligations with respect to the goods, including delivery of conforming documents related to the goods. This makes it clear that if the seller is to avoid a breach of the delivery obligation, he must ensure that the documents themselves conform to the goods in question. In this case, the seller's failure to deliver the conforming documents at the time and in the manner prescribed in the contract or by the trade, gives the buyer the right to reject the contract

[384] Article 283 Uniform Act; At Common Law, this is known as the right to cure. This was illustrated in the case of *Borrowman Phillips & Co. v Free & Hollis* (1878) 4 QBD 500.

[385] Article 281 UAGCL.

[386] Ferreri, Silvia, "Remarks Concerning the Implementation of the CISG by the Courts (The Seller's Performance and Article 35)", (2005–2006), 25 *Journal of Law and Commerce*, pp. 223–239, p. 232.

[387] Issa-Sayegh, Joseph et al., *OHADA Traitéet Actes Uniformes Commentés et Annotés,* 3rd edition, Juriscope, 2008, (discussing on former Article 224) p.291; This is the same position under Article 35 CISG.

[388] The Sale of Goods Act refers to the documents of title which have the same meaning as they have in the Factor Acts. Then, it lists the documents falling within its generic and makes it clear that they are documents used in the ordinary course of business as proof of the possession or control of goods.

and claim for damages.[389] In other words, the buyer's rejection of the non-conforming goods due to improper documents over the goods exposes the seller to an immediate action for payment of damages for breach of contract. With regard to the conformity of the documents, the general rule is that failure to deliver or delivery of non-conforming documents is treated in the same way as the delivery of non-conforming goods.[390] This is so because UAGCL treats documents as an essential part of the goods and therefore, any missing part of the goods opens an action for the buyer to reject or request for the re-tender of that missing item of the goods.[391]

However, it remains a fact that delivery of non-confirming documents is considered as material to the sale.[392] This is often the case when the goods are delivered to a buyer who intends to resell them but they were delivered without the vital documentary title contrary to the contract, although the seller in this case had knowledge of the importance of the documents of title of the goods. It may also be the case of the delivery of an engine which cannot be used without the documents (guidelines and usage notice of the goods). Unless otherwise agreed, the documents need be handed over only in exchange for payment, for *prima facie* payment and delivery are concurrent conditions[393] and here, the delivery obligation is satisfied by the furnishing of the documents. Even though the purpose of documents as understood under the UAGCL may be for the seller to arrange for the transportation of the goods typically to sales at distance,[394] the main consideration here is for the buyer to be entitled to obtain possession and have a legitimate right to use the goods for commercial purpose with respect to the type and place of business.[395]

Suspension of payment

The non-fulfilment by the seller of any obligation to tender goods of conformity to which the duty of payment is correlative entitles the buyerto

389 Article 282 UAGCL.

390 Akuété Pedro Santos & Jean Yado Toé, *OHADA Droit Commercial Général, Op. cit.*,p. 390.

391 Article 289 UAGCL.

392 Article 254 UAGCL; Article 1615 Civil Code; Issa-Sayegh, Joseph et al., *OHADA Traité et Actes Uniformes Commentés et Annotés, Op. cit.*, p. 290; Fenéon, Alain & Gomez, Jean-René, *OHADA-Harmonisation du Droit des Affaires, Droit Commercial Général- Commentaires*, Paris, Edition EDICEF, 1999, p.130; Bills of lading, warehouse warrants for instance have been acknowledged to be of relevance in modern sales.

393 Articles 262 & 267 UAGCL.

394 Article 252 UAGCL.

395 Articles 234 & 235 UAGCL.

suspend payment until the obligation has been performed. According to the UAGCL, the exact time the buyer has to pay is located at the time thereupon the seller makes available to him either the goods or the documents representing the goods.[396] In other words, payment and delivery must be made simultaneously.[397] Thus, otherwise agreed, payment and delivery are concurrent conditions, and the buyer need not tender payment unless and until the seller has properly performed his own obligations to the contract. This provision seems to secure both parties. It allows the seller to remain in control of the goods until the buyer pays and on the buyer's part, he will not proceed with the payment until delivery of the right goods. At times, payment of the price may be conditioned. Depending on the circumstances of each case, the seller may condition delivery of the goods or handing over of the documents on payment of the purchase price[398] or the buyer may condition payment of the price after examination of the goods.[399]

From this standpoint, it is therefore clear that both parties enjoy under these provisions the right of retention. To the buyer, it will all depend whether it is a paid or an unpaid seller as the case may be under Common law before he can exercise his right. The UAGCL has not expressly made such a distinction. In particular, the buyer's right of retention is evidenced by the fact that he will only release payment when the goods are placed at his disposal. Moreover, the buyer's right may sometimes be extended when he has to examine the goods before acceptance.[400] This situation evidently signifies that either physical possession or such form of constructive possession is a reasonable opportunity afforded the buyer to examine the goods.Also, in accordance with Article 272 of the Uniform Act, the buyer exercises an extended right of retention of title by keeping control over the undesired goods until the seller reimburses the expenses he incurred for their safety.[401] This is a typical condition for securing performance by the seller against retention of the goods. Moreover, if the contract of sale requires transportation of goods, the seller usually takes the risk to forward the goods to the buyer or through his agent with the related documents as well[402]. The buyer in this case may

---

[396] Article 266 UAGCL.

[397] This is a similar position at Common Law as per Sale of Goods Act, 1979, s 28.

[398] *Ibid*

[399] Article 267 para. 2 UGACL.

[400] Article 267 para. 2 UAGCL.

[401] Article 272 UGACL ; Akuété Pedro Santos & Jean Yado Toé, *OHADA Droit Commercial Général,Op. cit.*, p. 405; Ingebod Schwenzer, *Commentary on the UN Convention on the International Sale of Goods (CISG)*, (Schlechtriem & Schwenzer edition), Oxford University Press, 3rd edition., 2010, Mohs, paragraph 23–25, p. 852.

[402] Article 250 UAGCL.

decide to retain the documents and send back the goods to the seller in case he finds any defects in the goods. Such a measure is to hold the seller to act accordingly or reimburse any money paid representing the price of the goods. In other words, the title over the goods will be retained by the buyer until the goods are in conformity to the contract stipulation.

Reduction in price

Likewise, the buyer's right to reduce the price applies with respect to all the non-conforming goods, whether they have subsequently perished or not. If the goods do not conform to the contract, the buyer may reduce the price in the same proportion as the value that the goods actually delivered bears to the value that conforming goods would have had at that time.[403]This is regardless of whether it concerns a paid or an unpaid seller. However, the buyer shall only be entitled to damages and interests regarding the part(s) of the goods which are not in conformity.[404] This will depend if the buyer has accepted delivery of the parts which are in conformity. In other words, the buyer cannot be heard to claim damages where he had failed to notify the seller of his refusal to accept the tender of part(s) of the goods which are defective thereby holding them. He is entitled to ensure the safety of the goods until the seller reimburses the expenses he incurred for their safety.[405]In order to calculate how to reduce the price, courts need to interpret the two elements:

Firstly, the value of the goods actually delivered.[406] This would mean that the price of the goods accepted after delivery has been effected.[407]

Secondly, the value that conforming goods would have had. That is, this would be determined by the price agreed upon by the parties.[408]

Right to Damages: Damages to other Goods of the Buyer

Damages are one of the remedies available for breach of contract.[409] In the UAGCL and common law systems, the reason for awarding damages is to compensate, and nothing more. Damages for breach of contract usually aim

[403] Article 288 UAGCL; Mba-Owono, Charles, "Non-conformité et Vices Cachés dans la Vente Commerciale en Droit Uniforme Africain, *Op. cit.*, p.126; Malaurie, Philippe et al, *Droit Civil, Les Contrats Spéciaux, Op. cit.*, p.203.

[404] Article 289 UAGCL.

[405] Article 272–274 UAGCL.

[406] Article 292 para. 2 UAGCL; Section 2- 714 (2) of the UCC.

[407] Section 2–714 (2) of the UCC also contains the same meaning.

[408] Article 292 para. 1 UAGCL.

[409] Ewan McKendrick, *Contract Law, Op. cit*, p. 829.

to fulfill the aggrieved party's expectations by putting him into as good a position he would have been in if the contract had been properly performed.[410] In practice, the principle of full compensation under the UAGCL is meant to include all pecuniary losses that the aggrieved party would have incurred under the contract, in addition to all actual losses but for the breach.[411] The test is whether it is sufficient for the aggrieved party to prove that he has suffered non-performance from his counter party as a result of the breach or if he also has to prove that the loss was suffered as a consequence of the non-performance. Both tests will be used in the assessment of damages.

As a general rule under the Uniform Act, in matters of sale where an aggrieved party accepts and has been granted avoidance of the contract due to a serious breach of the duty of performance, his claim may give way to a request for payment of damages.[412] In this event, the buyer may claim damages for the seller's lack of conformity of goods. The measure of damages would be estimated on the loss directly and naturally resulting, in the ordinary course of event, from the breach of the contract, and in the case of breach of the warranty as to the quality of goods, this is *prima facie* the amount by which the value of the goods as contracted exceeds their value in the state in which they are delivered.

Damages may also be granted also when repair is made at the seller's expense, that is, the cost incurred to redress the defective goods.[413] For example, the buyer having received the conforming goods with delay[414] or the goods may be non-conforming; some costs may have been incurred by the buyer in the transportation of goods twice or for conserving the goods in a warehouse.[415]

Consequential loss claims may well arise upon the acceptance of the goods which prove defective. At common law, such claims will be governed by the rule laid down in the judgment of the case of *Hadley v. Baxendale*[416] whereby

[410] Andrew Burrows, *Op. cit.*, p.16; Pascal Nguihe Kante, "La Prise en Compte des Attentes Légitimes du Cocontractant en Droit Privé des Contrats", (2008) (12) *Annales de la Faculté des Scieces Juridiques et Politiques, Université de Dschang*, p.35; Nicholas B., *The French Law of Contract, Op. cit.*, p. 225. For tort, damages usually aim to put the plaintiff into as good a position as he would have been in if no tort had been committed. Whereas the payment of damages for a breach of a tort "is essential to the maintenance of the tort system as an effective, credible deterrent to negligence", without some kind of punishment for the defendant, there is no reason, other than a matter of conscience, for him not to commit that tort again. Providing the guilty party with a punishment is a way of deterring unsafe conduct.

[411] Akuété Pedros Santos & Jean Yado Toé, *Op. cit.*, p. 417.

[412] Article 281 UAGCL.

[413] Article 292 (1) and (2) UAGCL.

[414] With respect to Articles 258 and 259 UAGCL.

[415] Article 272 UAGCL.

[416] [1854] 9 Exch 341.

the measure of damages is the estimated loss directly and naturally resulting in an ordinary course of events from the buyer's breach.

Restitutionary Remedy

Unlike reliance interest, which focuses on the costs incurred by the non-breaching party, or expectation interest, which is concerned with the gains and losses that full performance of the contract would produced, restitution as a remedy for breach looks to the benefits conferred by one party on the other. Restitution's concept of "benefit," however, is elusive. It may be understood as requiring an increase in the wealth of the receiving party. In that event, one of the primary purpose of restitution is to avoid unjustly enriching one person at the expense of another.[417]

Restitution under the UAGCL is retroactive, which is the direct effect of the cancellation of the contract of sale.[418] In the first place, when a contracting party has either performed his obligations in whole or partially under the contract, in application of the rule of restitution, that party shall claim from the other party refund of what he had delivered or paid in performance of the contract.[419] A mutual restitution as such binds both parties, and not just the breaching party whose non-performance led to avoidance of the contract. As such, the effect of cancelling a contract of sale under the Uniform Act does not exonerate the parties from paying any damages due.[420] That is to say, each party must restore in return for restitution by the other.[421] As a consequence of the avoidance, the contract disappears as never existed between the parties. This restitution remedy is based on the net benefit conferred upon the breaching party by the victim. Thus, it is a routine element of restitutionary remedies for breach that the aggrieved party also must restore the value of any benefits received from the party in breach. Such mutual restoration as the case under the Uniform Act, might suggest that the goal of the restitution remedy for breach of contract is to return the aggrieved party to the *status quo ante.*[422]

It therefore appears that restitution may be partial. This may be due to the fact that the seller has partially performed his obligations or because of some

417 Eric G. Anderson, "The Restoration Interest and Damages for Breach of Contract", (1994), 53 *Maryland Law Review,* pp.1–64, p.6.

418 Joseph Issa-Sayegh, et al., *Traité et Actes Uniformes Commentés et Annotés, Op. cit.,* (Commenting on former Article 270 of the former Uniform Act) p. 300.

419 Article 297 UAGCL.

420 Article 296 UAGCL.

421 Article 269 UAGCL; Ingeborg Schwenzer, *Op. cit,* p .1106.

422 Eric G. Anderson, *Op. cit,* p. 6; Akuété Pedro Santos & Jean Yado Toé, *Op. cit.,* p. 415.

other reasons such as impossibility to perform, the buyer could take a legal action to recover what is due based on a restitutionary remedy.[423]

Once the recission of the contract is effective, restitution shall take place immediately so as to comply with the effect of avoidance, aimed at putting parties in the position they would have been had there never been a contract between them. In effect, it follows that there will be no restitution if there has not been performance by either contracting party. If there has been performance, by either both or one party, restitution may take place.

Strictly construed, the idea of restitution interest under the Uniform Act in returning the parties to their pre-contractual positions persists. It is expressed in the event where the goods expected to be restored must be refunded in the state in which the buyer had received them at the formation of the contract.[424] But if before the restitution the goods are no more available or are destroyed, the restitution will take place by money compensation.[425] The value of the goods shall be that the goods had at the making of the contract.[426]

The purpose of restitution under the Uniform Act is to prevent one party to the contract to unjustly be enriched against the other party who has performed his obligation under the contract. In order to avoid such a situation under the contract, the law requires the party who has received or benefited from performance, to compensate the other party's performance,[427] in addition to the benefit earned for the received performance.[428]

In addition, if there had been any expenses on the maintenance of the goods to be returned, the buyer who is the beneficiary of the restitution shall be compensated for such expenses incurred.[429] Also any expenses incurred by the buyer before restoring the goods shall be refunded. Otherwise, if the goods restored are defective, damages may be awarded to the aggrieved party.[430] However, in the event where the contract has been cancelled, the seller shall refund any interest gained from the price paid for the goods before restoration of the goods by the buyer.[431] It means, therefore, that parties are required to disclose all profits earned from the goods, as it shall be returned in compensation to the other party. The interest starts from the day of the payment thereof.

[423] Articles 281 para. 2, 282 & 296 UAGCL.
[424] Articles 283 & 298 UAGCL.
[425] Remy Cabrillac, *Droit des Obligations*, (7 édition, Dalloz, 2006) p. 80.
[426] Article 273 para.2 UAGCL.
[427] Article 297 UAGCL.
[428] Article 300 UAGCL.
[429] Article 272 UAGCL.
[430] Akuété Pedro Santos & Jean Yado Toé, *Op. cit.*, p. 415.
[431] Article 300 UAGCL.

Reliance Interest

The reliance interest takes its bearing from the "sunk costs" of the aggrieved party. When protected, it compensates a party for losses or harms that were incurred or suffered based on the assumption that the promise of the breaching party would be kept. The modern understanding of the reliance interest derives from the article by Fuller and Perdue, which generalised that it puts the injured party in the position he would have occupied had the contract not been formed, provided that the reliance damages do not exceed the expectation interest.[432]

Accordingly, it could be supposed that the purpose of awarding damages under the Uniform Act (though it is more of an expectation interest), is based on the claim of reliance interest in placing the aggrieved party in the position in which it would have been if he had not relied on the due performance of the contract.[433] For instance, where the contract of sale has ended and the buyer has made a purchase in replacement of the contract of the goods, or the seller has resold the goods, the buyer is entitled to claim damages on the basis of the difference between the contract price and the cost of the replacement or the resale. Thus, what may turn to be the expectancy interest of the buyer in reliance of the contract could be recoverable under a claim of reliance interest. With reference to conventional contract law, the buyer's reliance damages are protected, which are less than its expectation damages, because its profits cannot be proven with sufficient certainty.[434] As a result, the aggrieved party is put back to the position prior to the contract being made as opposed to the position as if the contract where successfully made. It therefore means that reliable interest is taken to be, "losses caused" *(damnum emergens),* and "gains prevented" (*lucrum cessans*) generally falls within the scope of the Uniform Act. In the first place, though reliance ordinarily results in "losses" of an affirmative nature (expenditure labour and money) it is also true that opportunities for gain may be forgone in reliance on a promise. Hence the reliance interest must be interpreted as at least potentially covering "gains prevented" as well as "losses caused". Obviously, certain scruples concerning "causality" and "foreseeable financial interest" which the aggrieved party would have regardless of the breach are suggested to constitute the reliance interest under the Uniform Act.[435] It is enough for present purpose to note

432 L.L. Fuller & William R. Perdue, "The Reliance Interest in Contract Damages", (1936) 40 (52) *Yale Law Journal,* pp. 1–27, p. 2.
433 Article 292 UAGCL; Akuété Pedro Santos & Jean Yado Toé, *Op. cit.*, p. 417.
434 Eric G. Anderson, "The Restoration Interest and Damages for Breach of Contract", *Op. cit.*, p. 6.
435 Akuété Pedro Santos & Jean Yado Toé, *Op. cit.*, p. 417.

that there is nothing in the definition of the reliance interest itself which would exclude items of this sort from consideration.

Expectation Interest

The contractual expectation interest traditionally is conceived in terms of a promisee's expectation of receiving the promised benefit of the contract.[436]It is, as a matter of fact, clear that the things which the law of damages purports to "measure" and "determine" – the "injuries" and to ascertain whether the plaintiff has included the "items of damage" in his complaint.[437]. One finds here the normal rule of contract damages which is expectation interest. This refers to the award to the promisee the value of the expectancy. The purpose of awarding expectation interest under the Uniform Act is generally to award profit to the buyer had it been that the seller had performed its delivery obligations.[438] In other words, this measure of awarding damages under the Uniform Act rotates around the idea a breach is deemed when it substantially deprives a party of the benefit that it is legitimately entitled to expect under the contract if the buyer had performed his own obligations. We can, to be sure, understand that the "compensation" here seems to be appropriate because the seller's breach deprived the buyer of the expectancy. Thus, it is convenient to say without any doubt that the Uniform Act is basically in favour of expectation interest than any other type of damages.

Thus, by way of explanation, the purport of expectation interest under the Uniform Act suggests that where the contract has been cancelled and the buyer has made a purchase in replacement of the goods or the seller has resold the goods, the buyer's damages shall be estimated from the difference between the contact price and the price of the replacement of the purchase or the resale, as well as all other damages to which it may be entitled. The aim of the Uniform Act is to put the buyer in as a good position as it would have occupied had the seller preformed his promise. The interest protected in this case is purely the expectation interest of the buyer. In his article, Professor Burton argues that expectation interest also encompasses the expected costs to the promisor, which consist of opportunities forgone at the time of contract formation. This cost perspective articulates an operational standard of good faith performance.[439]

[436] Steven J. Burton, "Breach of Contract and the Common Law Duty to Perform in Good Faith", (1980) 94 *Harvard Law Review*, p. 1.
[437] L.L. Fuller & William R. Perdue, "The Reliance Interest in Contract Damages", *Op. cit.*, p. 1.
[438] Article 292 UAGCL.
[439] Steven J. Burton, *Op. cit.*

A reason which may be advanced for the Uniform Act protecting the expectancy of the buyer may be found in the much -discussed "will theory" of contract law. This theory gives way for the agreement of contracting parties to be enforceable by the law. Thus, if any party to this contract violates any term, the law is there to compel the defaulting party to perform his obligations as set up by the parties. This theory reinforces the notion that every contract create a "right" which needs to be enforceable by the courts. Under such a rule, the penalty for violating the norm established by the contract would simply consist in being compelled to compensate the aggrieved party for detrimental reliance.

Again, from the economic standpoint, the Uniform Act can be appraised for protecting the expectation interest for purposes of the existing economic environment and to enhance the reliance on business agreements. Basically, the breach of a promise renders an actual diminution of the buyer's assets, in the sense that the latter had not "used" the property which the contract represents. Expectations of future values, become for commercial purposes, present values to the buyer,[440] because he needs it for possible or future commercial uses.

Conclusion:

This chapter reveals that the Uniform Act on General Commercial Law contains a comprehensive system of remedies for aggrieved buyers which pre-empts remedies available under domestic sales laws. This chapter has explored the consistent scheme set up by the Uniform Act in determining non-conformity and the remedies that the buyer can resort to in the case of non-conformity. Most remarkably, this chapter revisits the expectation and restitution interests; concepts that are instrumental in shaping our understanding of contract remedies embodied in the UAGCL in view to bring relief to the commercial buyer. A superior model is bipolar, with the expectation interest standing opposite the restoration interest. These two interests—one pulling toward the economic equivalence of full performance and the other toward the replication of the status quo—constitute the alternatives that determine the measure of damages for seller's lack of conformity under the OHADA Uniform Act on General Commercial Law. However, interest rates are also an additional compensation alongside

[440] L.L. Fuller & William R. Perdue, *Op. cit.*, p. 4.

payment of damages to the buyer where necessary.

The provisions of the Uniform Act on the seller's duty to cure must be appraised in the light of the policies and purposes they pursue. The policy underlying the Uniform Act's provisions is to link the duty to cure with the concept of conformity as well as with the burden of passing of risk, which must be approved for numerous reasons. It has been pointed out that, in certain circumstances, risk and delivery of conforming goods are dissociated, so that the buyer bears the risk while the goods are in conformity intended to be tendered to the buyer in accordance with the contract stipulations. But, the seller's duties under the Uniform Act to cure a defect in goods or to cure a non-conforming delivery are all encapsulated under the concept of conformity. The commercial buyer cares about the quality of goods in conformity with the contract terms for his business. It is therefore important for the seller to cure any defects in the goods before they are in the buyer's possession. The Uniform Act on General Commercial Law takes account of the dangers of such a situation, and Article 257 clearly provides that in such a case, the seller is under the obligation to cure the defects and tender conforming goods to the buyer. The Uniform Act has offered the seller possible means to cure a non-conforming delivery before and after delivery of the goods. Besides, the question of how the seller chooses to exercise this duty and the question of the fundamentality of such non-performance should be clearly treated separately by the Uniform Act. The task here appears to link the buyer's rejection of the goods where payment of the goods may have been effected by the buyer and the seller defaults in this duty to rightly deliver. This would represent a total failure of consideration by the seller and consequently, the buyer has a right of action on the contract. This calls for a clear distinction to be made under the Uniform Act between a paid and an unpaid seller so as to determine the extent of the buyer's right to claim for performance.

The commercial buyer places much interest to the quality of the goods to be delivered, which is essential for his resale business and as a matter of time, the seller's prompt action to cure is important. However, if the seller fails to protect the buyer's interest in curing any defects reported by the buyer, the Uniform Act provides the opportunity for the buyer to resort to other adequate remedies for the seller's non-conforming performance as a result of the seller's fundamental breach of contract.

BIBLIOGRAPHY

Books

Arthur Best & Alan R. Andreasen, *"Consumer Response to Unsatisfactory Purchase: A Survey of Perceiving Defects, Voicing Complaints, and Obtaining Redress",* (1977) 11 Law & Society, pp.701–742, p. 703.

Atiyah et al., *The Sale of Goods, 12th Edition, Longman,* Pitman Publishing, London, 2010, p.6.

Cheshire, Fifoot and Furmston, *Law of Contract* (14th edition, Butterworths, 2001), ch 13.

Etienne Nsie, *" La Formation de la Vente Commerciale en Afrique"* (1999) 829 *Penant.*

Fone Anne Marie,(1998) *"Le Secteur Informel Camerounais au regard du Doit Commercial",* Tome 2, Annales de la Facultés des Sciences Juridiques, Université de Dschang.

Friedrich Schneider & Dominik H. Enste, *Shadow Economies: Size, Causes, and Consequences,* 38 J. Econ. Lit. 77, 78–79 (2000).

G. H. Treitel, *Law of Contract* (11th edition, Sweet & Maxwell, London 2003), ch. 13.

Hugh Beale et al., *Cases, Materials and Text on Contract Law,* (Hart Publishing, 2002) p. 141.

J. Paul Peter & Jerry C. Olson, Consumer Behavior and Marketing Strategy.

Noel Thierry Kanchop, *Le Secteur Informel a l'Epreuve du Droit des Affaires OHADA,* Mémoire de D.E.A., Université de Dschang, 2008.

Paul Mitchell and John Phillips, *"Contractual Nexus: Is Reliance Essential?"* (2002) 22(1) *OJLS* 115.

Ingebod Schwenzer, *Commentary on the UN Convention on the International Sale of Goods (CISG),* (Schlechtriem & Schwenzer edition), Oxford University Press, 3rd Edition, 2010, Mohs, paragraph 23–25.

Remy Cabrillac, *Droit des Obligations,* (7 édition, Dalloz, 2006).

Fenéon, Alain & Gomez, Jean-René, *OHADA-Harmonisation du Droit des Affaires, Droit Commercial Général- Commentaires,* Paris, Edition EDICEF, 1999.

Issa-Sayegh, Joseph et al., *OHADA Traitéet Actes Uniformes Commentés et Annotés,* 3rd edition, Juriscope, 2008.

Leisinger, K. Benjamin, *Fundamental Breach—Considering Non-Conformity of the Goods,* Germany, European Law Publishers GmbH, 2007.

Ghestin, Jacques, *Conformité et Garanties dans la Vente (produits mobiliers),* Paris, LGDJ, 1983.

Furmston,, Michael, *Cheshire, Fifoot and Furmston's Law of Contract,* 12th Edition, Butterworths.

Martor, Boris et al, *Business Law in Africa, OHADA and the Harmonization Process,* London, GMB Publishing Ltd., 2nd edition, 2002.

Jean-Marie Nyama, *Eléments de Droit des Affaires Cameroun-OHADA,* (Presse de l'UCAC, Collection Apprendre, Yaoundé2002).

Pougoué, Paul-Gérard & Kalieu Elongo, Yvette Rachel, *Introduction Critique a l'OHADA,* Yaoundé, P.U.A., 2008.

Leisinger, K. Benjamin, *Fundamental Breach- Considering Non-Conformity of the Goods,* Germany, European Law Publishers GmbH, 2007

Malaurie, Philippe et al, *Droit Civil, Les Contrats Spéciaux,* 3e édition, Montchrestien, L.G.D.J.

Nguebou, Josette, *Le Droit Commercial Général dans l'Acte Uniforme OHADA,* Collection Droit Uniforme OHADA, Yaoundé, P.U.A.

G.H. Treitel, The *Law of Contract,* 10th Edition, London, Sweet & Maxwell, 1999.

Harris, Donald & Denis, *Contract Law Today Anglo-French Comparisons,* Oxford, Clarendon Press, 1989.

Akuété Pedro Santos and Jean YadoToé, *OHADA Droit Commercial Général,* Collection Droit Uniforme Africain, Bruxelles, 2002.

J. Ademola Yakubu, *Law of Contract in Nigeria,* Mathouse Press Limited, 2003.

Goode, Roy, *Commercial Law,* 3rd Edition, Penguin Books, 2004.

Bradgate, Robert, *Commercial Law,* 3rd edition, Oxford University Press, 2005.

Akuété Pedros Santos & Jean YadoToé, *OHADA Droit Commercial Général,* Bruxelles, Bruylant, Collection Droit Uniforme Africain, 2002.

Burrows, Andrew, *Torts and Breach of Contract*, 2nd Edition, London, Butterworths, 1994.

Henri &Leon Mazeaud et al., *Obligations, théorie générale, Leçons De Droit Civil,*(9 Ed., Montchrestien,1998).

Hugh Beale et al., *Cases, Materials and Text on Contract Law,*(Hart Publishing, 2002) p.141.

Michael Furmston, *Law of Contract, Law of Contract,* (14thedition, Butterworths, 2001.

Cheshire, Fifoot and Furmston, *Law of Contract* (14thedition, Butterworths, 2001).

Atiyah et al., *The Sale of Goods,* 12th Edition, Longman, Pitman Publishing, London, 2010.

N.E. Simmonds, *Central Issues in Jurispudence, Justice, Law and Rights* (2nd edition, Sweet & Maxwell, London) 2002, pp.304–307.

Michael J. Trebilock, *The Limits of Freedom of Contract* (Havard University Press, 1993).

Articles

Larry Dimatteo *et al.*, "The Interpretive Turn in International Sales Law: An Analysis of Fifteen Years of CISG Jurisprudence", (2004) 24 *Northwestern Journal of International Law and Business*, pp. 299–392, p. 292.

S. Todd Lowry, "*Bargain and Contract Theory in Law and Economics*", (1976) 10 (1) *Journal of Economic Issues*, pp. 1–22.

Fiona M. Scott Morton in his article the *Cato Review of Business and Government*. (Vol. 24, No. 1, 2001).

Taiwo A. Oriola,"*Consumer Dilemmas:The Right to Know, Safety, Ethics and Policy of Genetically Modified Food*",(2002) *Singapore Journal of Legal Studies*, pp. 514–573.

Robert C. Brown, "*The Liability of Retail Policies for Defective Food Products*",

(1939) 23 *Minnesota Law Review*, pp. 585–611.

G. J. Stigler, "*The Economics of Information*", (1961) 69 *Journal of Political Economy.*

Priest, Breach and Remedy for the Tender of Non conforming Goods under the Uniform Commercial Code: An Economic Approach, (1978) 91 *Harvard Law Review* 960.

Jean Claude James, "*La Vente Commerciale OHADA, Précurseur d'*un Droit Harmonisé des Contrats?", Actes du Colloque International de Libreville sur *"Les Pratiques Contractuelles d'Affaires et les Processus d'Harmonisation dans les Espaces Régionaux"*, Octobre 26–28, 2011, pp. 26–48

Ferreri, Silvia, "*Remarks Concerning the Implementation of the CISG by the Courts (The Seller's Performance and Article 35)*", (2005–2006), 25 *Journal of Law and Commerce*, pp. 223–239.

Samgena D. Galega, "*Strict Liability for Defective Products in Cameroon? Some Illuminating Lessons from Abroad*", 48 (2) Journal of African Law, pp. 239–270, p. 253.

Antonio J. Senagore, "*The Benefits of Limiting Strict Liability for Used-Product Sellers*", (2010) 30 *Northern Illinois University Law Review*, pp.1–34, p. 3.

Erauw, Johan, "*CISG Articles 66–70: The Risk of Loss and Passing It*", (2005) 25 *Journal of Law and Commerce*, pp.1–13.

Ferreri, Silva, "*Remarks Concerning the Implementation of the CISG by the Courts. (The Seller's Performance and Article 35)*", (2005–2006) 25, *Journal of Law and Commerce*, pp.224–225.

Schneider, Eric C., "*The Seller's Right to Cure under the Uniform Commercial Code and the United Nations Convention Code on Contract for the International Sale of Goods*", (1989) *7 Arizona Journal of International and Comparative Law*, pp. 1–27.

Flechner, Harry M., "*Buyers' Remedies in General and Buyers' Performance-Oriented Remedies*", (2005–2006) 25 (339) *Journal of Law and Commerce*, pp. 339–347, p. 343.

Gomez, Jean René, "*Un Nouveau Droit de la Vente Commerciale en Afrique*", (1999) *Revue Penant*, pp. 145–185.

Ingeborg Schwenzer, "*Buyer's* Remedies in the case of Non-Conforming: Some Problems in a core area of the CISG", (2007)101 *Am. Soc'y Int'll Proc.* 416.

Anne-Catherine Imhoff-Scheier, *Protection du Consommateur et Contrats Internationaux, (*Librairie de L'Université George & Cie S.A., Genève 2002).

Mba-Owono, Charles, "*Non-conformité et Vices Cachés dans la Vente Commerciale en Droit Uniforme Africain*", (2000) 41 *Juridis Périodique*, pp.107–127.

Claire Moore Dickerson, "*Bringing Formal Business Laws to Cameroon's Informal Set or: Lessons and Cautious from the Tax Law Example*", (2014) 13 *Washington University Global Study Law Review* 265, pp. 1–42, p. 3.

Steven J. Burton, "*Breach of Contract and the Common Law Duty to Perform in Good Faith*", (1980) 94 *Harvard Law Review.*

L.L. Fuller & William R. Perdue, "*The Reliance Interest in Contract Damages*", (1936) 40 (52) *Yale Law Journal,* pp. 1–27.

Eric G. Anderson, "*The Restoration Interest and Damages for Breach of Contract*", (1994), 53 *Maryland Law Review,* pp.1–64.

Pascal Nguihe Kante, "*La Prise en Compte des Attentes Légitimes du Cocontractant en Droit Privé des Contrats*", (2008) (12) *Annales de la Faculté des Sciences Juridiques et Politiques, Université de Dschang.*

Fone Anne Marie,(1998) "*Le Secteur Informel Camerounais au regard du Doit Commercial*", Tome 2, *Annales de la Facultés des Sciences Juridiques,* Université de Dschang.

Claire Moore Dickerson, *Informal-Sector Entrepreneurs, Development and Formal Law: A Functional Understanding of Business Law,* 59 Am. J. Comp. L. 179, 185 (2011).

Friedrich Schneider & Dominik H. Enste, *Shadow Economies: Size, Causes, and Consequences,* 38 *J. Econ. Lit.* 77, 78–79 (2000).

Roland Djieufack & Irene Fokum Sama-lang, "*From Caveat Emptor to Caveat Venditor- An Assessment of Conformity of Goods to the Contract of Sale under the Uniform Act on General Commercial Law: A Contract Law Perspective*", (*International Journal of Law and Policy Review [IJLPR]).*

Franklin E. Crawford, "*Fit for its Ordinary Purpose? Tobacco, Fast Food, and the Implied Warranty of Merchantability*", (2002) 63 *Ohio State Law Journal*, 1165.

Peter H. Schlectreim, "*Non-Material Damages - Recovery under the CISG?*", (2007) Reproduced with permission of 19 *Pace International Law Review*, p. 89–102.

Arthur Best & Alan R. Andreasen, "*Consumer Response to Unsatisfactory Purchase: A Survey of Perceiving Defects, Voicing Complaints, and Obtaining Redress*", (1977) 11 *Law & Society*, pp.701–742.

Antonio J. Senagore, "*The Benefits of Limiting Strict Liability for Used-Product Sellers*", (2010) *30 Northern Illinois University Law Review*, pp.1–34.

J. Paul Peter & Jerry C. Olson, *Consumer Behavior and Marketing Strategy*, (2nd edition, Homewood 1998) pp. 496–510.

Adam M. Giuliano, "*Nonconformity in the Sale of Goods between the United States and China*: The New Chinese Contract Law, the Uniform Commercial Code, and the Convention on Contracts for the International Sale of Goods," (2006) 18 *Florida Journal of International Law*, 331.

Theses/Dissertations

Noel Thierry Kanchop, *Le Secteur Informel a l'Epreuve du Droit des Affaires OHADA*, Mémoire de D.E.A., Université de Dschang, 2008.

Edie Diable Pascal, *Contract of Sale of Goods under the OHADA Uniform Act on General Commercial Law, The Common Law and the CISG: A Comparative Study*, (Masters Dissertation, Faculty of Law and Political Science, University of Dschang, 2011)